Nick Vandome

Windows 10

2nd edition
Updated for the Windows 10 Anniversary Update

In easy steps is an imprint of In Easy Steps Limited
16 Hamilton Terrace · Holly Walk · Leamington Spa
Warwickshire · United Kingdom · CV32 4LY
www.ineasysteps.com

Second Edition

In Easy Steps Limited supports The Forest Stewardship Council (FSC),
the leading international forest certification organization. All our titles
that are printed on Greenpeace approved FSC certified paper carry the
FSC logo.

MIX
Paper from
responsible sources
FSC® C020837

Printed and bound in the United Kingdom

ISBN 978-1-84078-751-1

Contents

8 Digital Lifestyle 159

9 Microsoft Edge Browser 177

10 Keeping in Touch 195

Networking 209

System and Security 221

Index 233

1 Introducing Windows 10

This chapter explains what Windows is and shows how to get started with the operating system, including the changes in Windows 10 and its interface, keyboard shortcuts, creating a Microsoft Account and signing in.

What is Windows?

Windows is an operating system for PCs (personal computers), laptops and smartphones. The operating system is the software that organizes and controls all of the components (hardware and software) in your computer so that they integrate and work efficiently together.

The first operating system from Microsoft was known as MS-DOS (Microsoft Disk Operating System). This was a non-graphical, line-oriented, command-driven operating system, able to run only one application at a time.

The original Windows system was an interface manager that ran on top of the MS-DOS system, providing a graphical user interface and using clever processor and memory management to allow it to run more than one application or function at a time.

The basic element of Windows was its 'windowing' capability. A window (with a lower-case w) is a rectangular area used to display information or to run a program. Several windows can be opened at the same time so that you can work with multiple applications. This provided a dramatic increase in productivity, in comparison with the original MS-DOS.

Microsoft released four versions of this interface management Windows, with numerous intermediate versions, including:

- 1985 – Windows 1.0; 1987 – Windows 2.0, 2.1 and 2.11; 1990 – Windows 3.0, 3.1, 3.11 (Windows for Workgroups); 1995 – Windows 95; 1998 – Windows 98, 98 SE; 2000 – Windows Me (Millennium Edition).

The next version, Windows XP, was a full operating system in its own right. This was eventually followed by Windows Vista and then Windows 7, 8, 8.1 and 10 (there was no Windows 9).

- 2001 – Windows XP (eXPerience) Home and Professional.

- 2007 – Windows Vista Home, Home Premium, Ultimate etc.

- 2009 – Windows 7 Starter, Home Premium, Ultimate etc.

- 2012 – Windows 8 Starter, Pro, Enterprise and RT.

- 2013 – Windows 8.1 Starter, Pro, Enterprise and RT.

- 2015 – Windows 10 Home, Pro, Enterprise and Education.

The New icon pictured above indicates a new or enhanced feature introduced with the Windows 10 Anniversary Update.

About Windows 10

The latest version of Windows was released in August 2016:

- 2016 – Windows 10 Anniversary Update, which can be used to upgrade any existing version of Windows 10.

All major computer operating systems (OS) undergo regular upgrades and new versions. Sometimes these are a significant visual overhaul, while others concentrate more on the behind-the-scenes aspect of the OS. In terms of Microsoft Windows, Windows 8 was one of the most radical updates to the User Interface (UI) and introduced a number of new features, for both desktop and mobile versions of Windows. However, it was not met with universal approval, as it was perceived that it was two separate operating systems (desktop and mobile) bolted together and not satisfying each environment completely.

With Windows 10, a lot of the problems with Windows 8 were addressed: the familiar Start menu was reinstated to return to a similar UI to earlier versions of Windows; there was a greater consolidation between desktop and mobile devices running Windows 10; and the operation of apps was standardized so that it is similar for the new Windows apps and also the more traditional ones. In a sense, this was a case of going back one step in order to go forwards two steps and Windows 10 has succeeded in creating a familiar environment, coupled with a range of innovative and useful features.

Windows 10 Anniversary Update

The intention for Windows 10 has always been to produce incremental updates, rather than waiting a period of time for the next major update. This is the reason why it is unlikely that there will be a Windows 11: instead there will be regular online updates to Windows 10. The Windows 10 Anniversary Update marks the first anniversary of the release of the software. It contains a number of improvements and refinements but, in keeping with the Windows 10 ethos, it is an incremental update rather than a major new operating system. The Anniversary Update is delivered online through the Windows Update function in the Settings app. A registered version of Windows 10 has to be installed in order for the Anniversary Update to be downloaded. Some of the new features in the update include an improved Start menu and improvements to the digital assistant, Cortana.

If you are upgrading to Windows 10 from Windows 7, 8 or 8.1 you will be able to keep all of your settings, files and apps.

The functionality of the Anniversary Update is generally the same as for the original Windows 10 and it will, in general, be referred to as Windows 10 throughout the book.

Windows 10 Interface

Windows 8 was one of the most significant changes to the Windows operating system since Windows 95 helped redefine the way that we look at personal computers. It aimed to bring the desktop and mobile computing environments together, principally with the brightly colored Start screen and Charms bar. However, this proved to be awkward for a lot of users, with Windows 8 not fully meeting the needs of the device being used.

The original Windows 10 interface was redesigned so that it looked as similar as possible, regardless of whether it is being used on a desktop computer with a mouse and keyboard, or on a mobile or touchscreen device (and most of the underlying functionality is still the same). The Windows 10 Anniversary Update keeps the same interface, while adding some visual updates, such as an improved Start menu, and some internal improvements to ensure that Windows 10 runs more efficiently.

As with the original Windows 10, the Anniversary Update looks more familiar to users of pre-Windows 8 versions of Windows. It opens at the Desktop, where shortcuts to items can be placed, and the Taskbar is at the bottom of the screen. The Start screen format and the Charms bar have also been replaced with more traditional elements of the Windows operating system, including the enhanced Start menu.

The main recommended specifications for PCs and laptops running Windows 10 are: 1GHz processor; 1GB RAM (32-bit Windows) or 2GB RAM (64-bit Windows); and 16GB of free disk space for installation.

Start menu

The Start menu was reinstated in the original version of Windows 10, although it has been redesigned so that it also includes a range of colored tiles, which can be pinned to the Start menu and are used to access the most commonly used or favorite apps. The left-hand side of the Start menu contains links to some of your most frequently used functions (such as the Power button), Recently Added apps, Most used apps and the All Apps list. The Windows 10 Anniversary Update version refines the Start menu so that all apps are displayed directly on the menu, rather than having to be accessed from the All Apps button that appeared on the original version of Windows 10.

The Settings app can be used to customize the Start menu (**Settings** > **Personalization** > **Start**).

Windows 10 for touchscreen

The Windows 10 version that is optimized for touchscreen use is designed for using with a tablet (such as the Microsoft Surface Pro 4), where all of the screen navigation can be done by  tapping, swiping and pinching on the screen. These features can also be used on touchscreen desktops and laptops that have this functionality (see page 15 for details).

The Demise of the Charms Bar

One of the features in Windows 8 and 8.1 that did not meet with universal approval was the Charms bar. This was a bar of icons that appeared at the right-hand side of the screen when the cursor was moved to certain positions. The Charms bar consisted of: a Settings Charm, which was used for quick settings, including the Power button and the full PC Settings; a Device Charm for adding external devices; a Sharing Charm; and a Search Charm.

In the Windows 10 Anniversary Update, the Charms bar remains removed and its functionality has been incorporated into other features:

Don't forget

In Windows 8 and 8.1 the PC Settings were accessed from the Charms bar. The Settings in Windows 10 can be accessed from a range of locations, including the Start menu and the Notifications panel. See page 44 for details.

12

- **Power button**. This is available on the Start menu, which is accessed from the Start button in the bottom left-hand corner of the screen.

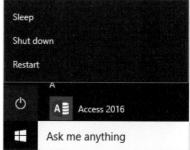

- **Notifications** and **Quick access settings**. These are available from the Notifications button at the right-hand side of the Taskbar, at the bottom of the Desktop. (This is also known as the Action Center.)

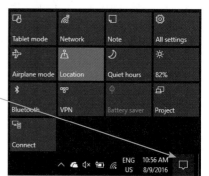

- **Search**. This is incorporated into the Taskbar, to the right of the Start button. It also includes the Cortana search function which is accessed from the microphone icon.

- **Device** and **Sharing** options. These are now incorporated into the menu within some of the modern Windows 10 apps. Click on the menu to access the options.

Obtaining Windows 10

Windows 10 is a slight departure by Microsoft in that it is promoted as an online service, rather than just a standalone operating system. This means that, by default, Windows 10 is obtained and downloaded online, with subsequent updates and upgrades provided on a regular basis.

The original version of Windows 10 was a free upgrade if it was downloaded and installed by July 2016. However, this offer has now finished and Windows 10 can be bought from the Microsoft website, or through software retailers. A registered version of Windows 10 has to been installed before the free Anniversary Update can be downloaded.

The three main options for obtaining Windows 10 are:

- **Upgrade** – Replace an older version of Windows, retaining the installed applications and settings. This can only be done with Windows 7 and later: for earlier versions you will need to install a new, full copy of Windows 10.

- **Clean Install** – This has to be done if you have Windows XP or Windows Vista and you want to upgrade to Windows 10.

- **Pre-install** – Buy a new PC or laptop with Windows 10 already installed, then install the required apps.

For users of Windows 7, 8 or 8.1, Windows 10 has to be installed before the Anniversary Update can be downloaded and installed from the Microsoft website. Ensure Windows Update is turned on within Settings to ensure you are informed about the update. Once it has been installed, you will receive upgrades and updates as they become available.

Some of the steps that the installation will go through are:

- **Personalize**. These are settings that will be applied to your version of Windows 10. These settings can also be selected within the Settings app once Windows 10 has been installed.

- **Settings**. You can choose to have express settings applied, or customize them.

- **Microsoft Account**. You can set up a Microsoft Account during installation, or once you have started Windows 10.

Don't forget

The cost for Windows 10, with a DVD, is US$119 (£99) for the Home edition.

Keyboard Shortcuts

As you become more confident using Windows 10 you may want to access certain items more quickly. There is a range of keyboard shortcuts that can be used to access some of the items you use most frequently.

The majority of the shortcuts are accessed together with the WinKey. To use the keyboard shortcuts press:

- **WinKey** to access the Start menu at any time

- **WinKey** + **L** to lock the computer and display the Lock screen

- **WinKey** + **I** to access the Settings app

- **WinKey** + **K** to connect new devices

- **WinKey** + **H** to access the Sharing options for the current items or app

- **WinKey** + **Q** to access the Personal Digital Assistant voice function, Cortana

- **WinKey** + **D** to access the Desktop

- **WinKey** + **M** to access the Desktop with the active window minimized

- **WinKey** + **E** to access File Explorer, displaying the Quick access section

- **WinKey** + **T** to display the thumbnails on the Desktop Taskbar

- **WinKey** + **U** to access the Ease of Access Center

- **WinKey** + **X** to access administration tools and quick access to items including the Desktop and the Control Panel

- **Alt** + **F4** to close a Windows 10 app

- **Ctrl** + **Shift** + **Esc** to access the Task Manager

Windows 10 for Touch

One of the aims of Windows 10 is to make the operating system more familiar again to users with a keyboard and mouse. This has been done by reverting back to a more traditional look and feel than that of Windows 8 and 8.1. For touchscreen devices such as tablets, laptops with precision touchpads and phones, the same overall operation of Windows 10 has been maintained so that users can feel comfortable with the operating system regardless of the device on which they are using it.

Continuum

Continuum refers to the function of Windows 10 where you can start something on one Windows 10 device and then continue working on it on another. For instance, you could start a letter in Word on a desktop computer, save it, and then pick up where you left off on the Microsoft tablet, Surface. Continuum works between desktop computers, laptops, tablets and Windows phones.

Using touch

Touchscreen devices and those with precision touchpads can be used with Windows 10 to navigate through a number of gestures, swipes and taps on the screen or touchpad. The range of these gestures has been consolidated from Windows 8 and 8.1, since these included a number of options for accessing the Charms that are no longer available with Windows 10. Some of the gestures that can be used with touchscreen or touchpad devices using Windows 10 are:

- Swipe inwards from the right-hand edge to access the Action Center (Notification Center).

- Swipe inwards from the left-hand edge to access the Task View for currently open apps.

- In an open Windows 10 app, swipe downwards from the top of the screen to access the app's toolbar.

- In an open Windows 10 app, use a long swipe downwards from the top of the screen to close the app.

- Swipe upwards from the bottom of the screen to access the Taskbar (when an app is at full screen).

- Tap with three fingers on a touchpad to bring up the Personal Digital Assistant, Cortana.

The Windows 10 Anniversary Update has enhanced Windows Ink, which enables users of a touchscreen device to jot down notes, make sketches and launch some apps, using a compatible pen.

Aside from the gestures used on a touchscreen device, much of the operation of Windows 10 has been consolidated between computers with a mouse and keyboard, and mobile devices.

Using a Microsoft Account

We live in a world of ever-increasing computer connectivity, where users expect to be able to access their content wherever they are and share it with their friends and family in a variety of ways, whether it is by email, messaging or photo sharing. This is known as Cloud computing, with content being stored on online servers, from where it can be accessed by authorized users.

In Windows 10, this type of connectivity is achieved with a Microsoft Account. This is a registration system (which can be set up with most email addresses and a password) that provides access to a number of services via the Windows 10 apps. These include:

Without a Microsoft Account you will not be able to access the full functionality of the apps listed here.

- **Mail**. This is the Windows 10 email app that can be used to access and manage your different email accounts.

- **Skype**. This is the text messaging and video chatting app.

- **People**. This is the address book app.

- **Calendar**. This is the calendar and organizer app.

- **Windows Store**. This is the online store for previewing and downloading additional apps.

- **OneDrive**. This is the online backup and sharing service.

Creating a Microsoft Account

It is free to create a Microsoft Account and can be done with an email address and, together with a password, this provides a unique identifier for logging into your Microsoft Account and the related apps. There are several ways in which you can create and set up a Microsoft Account:

- During the initial setup process when you install Windows 10. You will be asked if you want to create a Microsoft Account at this point. If you do not, you can always do so at a later time.

- When you first open an app that requires access to a Microsoft Account. When you do this you will be prompted to create a new account.

- From the **Accounts** section of the **Settings** app (for more information about the Settings app see pages 44-55).

...cont'd

Whichever way you use to create a Microsoft Account, the process is similar:

1 When you are first prompted to sign in with a Microsoft Account you can enter your account details, if you have one, or

Add your Microsoft account

Sign in with your Microsoft account. You can use this account with other apps on this device. Learn more.

someone@example.com

Password

Forgot my password

No account? Create one!

2 Click on the **No account? Create one!** link

No account? Create one!

Hot tip

3 Enter your name, an email address and a password for your Microsoft Account

Let's create your account

Windows, Office, Outlook.com, OneDrive, Skype, Xbox. They're all better and more personal when you sign in with your Microsoft account.* Learn more

Nick | Vandome

✓ After you sign up, we'll send you a message with a link to verify this user name.

nickvandome2@gmail.com

Get a new email address

••••••••

United States

Birth month | Day | Year

Back | Next

Microsoft Account details can also be used as your sign-in for Windows 10 (see pages 18-19).

17

4 Click on the **Next** button to move through the registration process

Next

5 Enter your password again to confirm your account

6 Click on the **Finish** button in the final window to complete setting up your Microsoft Account

Make it yours

Windows is better when your settings and files automatically sync. If you make nickvandome2@gmail.com your primary account, Windows will use it automatically with your Microsoft services, and for signing in to your device.

To make nickvandome2@gmail.com your primary account, we'll need your Windows password one last time to make sure it's really you.

Your Windows password

I'll connect my Microsoft account later.

Next

Sign-in Options

Each time you start up your computer you will need to sign in. This is a security feature so that no-one can gain unauthorized access to your account on your PC. The sign-in process starts with the Lock screen and then you have to enter your sign-in password.

Don't forget

For details about personalizing the Lock screen see pages 42-43.

1 When you start your PC the Lock screen will be showing. This is linked to the sign-in screen

10:50

Wednesday, July 29

Hot tip

You can lock your PC at any point by pressing **WinKey** + **L**.

2 Click on the **Lock screen**, or press any key to move to the sign-in screen. Enter your password and press **Enter** or click on this arrow

Nick Vandome
nickvandome@gmail.com

Don't forget

You will get an error message if you enter the wrong password or if you simply mis-key and cause an incorrect character to be added.

3 On the sign-in screen, click on this button to select Ease of Access options

4 On the sign-in screen, click on this button to select Power off options including Shut down and Restart

5 If there are other users with an account on the same PC, their names will be displayed here

 6 Click on another user to access their own sign-in screen

Sign-in settings

Settings for how you sign in can be accessed from the Accounts section in the Settings app:

1 Access the **Settings** app and click on the **Accounts** button

2 Under **Sign-in options**, select options to change your password, create a picture password or create a PIN instead of a password

3 If you want to create a picture password you must have a touchscreen device. Select a picture and draw a pattern to use as your sign-in

Don't forget

You can sign in with a Local account or a Microsoft Account. If you sign in with the latter, you will have access to the related services, such as Mail and People. Also, you will be able to sync your settings and use them on another computer when you log in with your Account.

Don't forget

For details about using the Settings app see pages 44-55.

Hot tip

Windows Hello is a function that uses biometric authentication for signing in to Windows 10. This is either done by scanning your face or with a fingerprint reader. However, specialist hardware is required and this is not available on many devices at present.

19

32-Bit versus 64-Bit

As well as choosing your Windows 10 edition, you also need to decide between the 32-bit and the 64-bit versions of the operating system. This choice is available for all editions of Windows 10, including installation DVDs for each mode.

The 32-bit or 64-bit nomenclature refers to the memory address length which the processor can reference. This dictates the maximum amount of memory, which is 4GB for 32-bit mode (or more accurately 3.4GB, since some memory needs to be allocated for other purposes). For 64-bit mode, the maximum may be much higher, though the Windows 10 editions do not make full use of the potential. As well as more memory, 64-bit mode will also be faster; typically about 10%.

However, you need applications that are specifically optimized for 64-bit processing to take advantage of the speed improvements and memory increase. Many games, for example, include the necessary enhancements.

Remember that choosing a 64-bit system means that you can no longer run 16-bit applications. This is only a problem if you use very old software (from the Windows 3.1 days).

More importantly, existing 32-bit drivers for your devices will not operate in 64-bit mode, so you will have to locate 64-bit versions of the drivers. You may have problems with some devices, particularly the older ones.

You may also find that running 32-bit applications in a 64-bit operating system might actually be slower, due to the additional overheads imposed by conversion between the address systems.

In summary, if you have a 64-bit capable computer but use older hardware or 32-bit applications, you might do better to stay with the 32-bit version of Windows 10. With the latest hardware and drivers, and applications that are 64-bit optimized, for especially demanding applications such as video editing or image packages, the switch to 64-bit and higher memory would offer significant improvements.

It will not be long before 64-bit computing becomes the standard, and 32-bit operation becomes an optional extra, but for the present there are still large numbers of 32-bit applications.

Hot tip

To check whether your version of Windows 10 is 32-bit or 64-bit, right-click on the Start button and click on the **System** link. The bit version is displayed under the **System** > **System type** section.

2 Getting Started

Windows 10 improves upon the radical design of Windows 8 and returns to a lot of the more traditional elements of Windows, such as the Start menu. This chapter looks at some of the main features of Windows 10, focusing on the redesigned Start menu and using the Desktop and the Taskbar. It also covers the Personal Digital Assistant, Cortana, for voice searching over your computer and setting reminders for a range of items.

The Start Button

When the predecessor to Windows 10 (Windows 8) was introduced there was a significant outcry due to the disappearance of the traditional Windows Start button. This was made worse by the removal of the Start menu too. However, the Start button was reinstated in Windows 8.1 and the Start menu has now also returned, in an enhanced format. This means that Windows 10 can be used in a similar way to traditional versions of Windows.

Using the Start button

The Start button provides access to the apps on your Windows 10 PC and also to the enhanced Start menu:

Hot tip

The items on the Start menu can be customized from the **Personalization** > **Start** section of the Settings app.

Hot tip

Click on the **Power** button on the Start menu to access options for Sleep, Shut down or Restart.

1 Click on the **Start** button in the bottom left-hand corner of the screen

2 The **Start** menu is displayed

3 The left-hand side of the Start menu contains links to frequently used apps, a list of quick links to items such as the Power button, and an alphabetic list of all of the apps on the computer

4 The right-hand side of the Start menu is where apps can be pinned so that they are always available. This is displayed as a collection of large, colored tiles

5 Other items can also be accessed from the Start button by right-clicking on it

Start button functionality

Although the Start button is different to earlier versions of Windows, it still has a range of functionality:

 1 Right-click on the **Start** button to view its menu

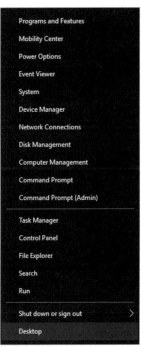

The Start button menu in Step 1 has a number of options for accessing system functions, such as Command Prompt and Disk Management.

 2 Click on the relevant buttons to view items including the **Desktop** and **Control Panel**

The view for the Control Panel can be changed by clicking the **View by** drop-down list at the top-right of the window. The options are Category, Large icons and Small icons. For the examples in the book, Category is used.

3 Shut down options are also available from the **Start** button (see page 33)

The Start Menu

The reinstated Start menu in Windows 10 is where you can access areas within your computer, perform certain functions and also access apps from a variety of locations. Some of the default items on the Start menu can be customized to a certain extent (see pages 26-27) and there is considerable functionality here:

 Click here to access the most recently installed or downloaded apps

 Your most frequently used apps are displayed here. Click on one to open it (these items will change as you use different apps)

 Click here to access your own account settings or sign out from your account

In previous versions of Windows 10 the Start menu contained an **All Apps** button. In the Anniversary Update, this has been replaced with the alphabetic list of all of the apps on the PC.

Recently added
Feedback Hub
Connect
McAfee Security Scan Plus
Most used
Mozilla Firefox
LibreOffice Writer
Adobe InDesign CS5
Snagit 11
PowerPoint 2016
Adobe Reader XI
#
3D Builder
A
Access 2016
Acer
Ask me anything

4 Click here to access items including the **File Explorer**, your **Documents** library within File Explorer and the Windows 10 **Settings**

5 Click on the **Power** button for options to **Sleep** your computer, **Shut down** or **Restart**

Sleep

Shut down

Restart

Access

Acer

Use the scroll bar at the right-hand side to move through the list of apps

Hot tip

Click on a letter at the top of a section of apps to view an alphabetic grid. Click on a letter to move to that section.

7 If there is a down-pointing arrow next to an app, this means that there are additional items that can be accessed. Click on the arrow to view these

Adobe Design Premium CS5

Customizing the Start Menu

Windows 10 is very adaptable and can be customized in several ways, so that it works best for you. This includes the Start menu which can be set to behave in certain ways and have specific items added to it. To do this:

1 Open the **Settings** app and click on the **Personalization** button

Personalization
Background, lock screen, colors

2 Click on the **Start** button

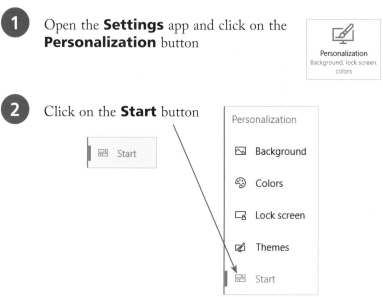

Personalization

Background

Colors

Lock screen

Themes

Start

Beware

Full screen mode is designed more for tablets, and if you use it, the Start menu will occupy the whole screen.

3 Under **Preview**, select whether to show suggestions for apps in the Start menu, show most used apps or recently used apps on the Start menu or show the Start menu full screen

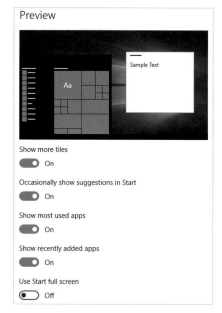

Preview

Show more tiles
On

Occasionally show suggestions in Start
On

Show most used apps
On

Show recently added apps
On

Use Start full screen
Off

4 Click on the **Choose which folders appear on Start** button to select the items that appear on the Start menu

5 Drag the buttons **On** or **Off** for the items you want to appear on the Start menu, i.e. the File Explorer, the Settings app and the Music app

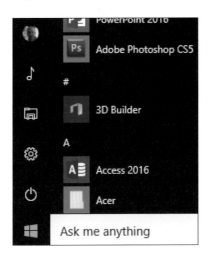

Don't forget

If you find that you do not use some items very much once they have been added to the Start menu, they can be removed by dragging their buttons to **Off** in Step 5.

6 The items selected in Step 5 appear on the Start menu, above the Power button

27

Working with Groups

By default, the apps on the Start menu are arranged in groups, such as Everyday apps. However, apps can be arranged into other groups, and new ones can also be created, by dragging apps between groups. To do this:

 Click and hold on a tile and drag it into another group to place it here. If there is no space, the other apps will move to accommodate the new one

Don't forget

If a group is moved on the Start menu, its name moves with it.

 Drag the tile into an empty space to create a new group

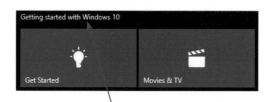

Don't forget

Depending on your geographic location, some terms will appear with alternative spellings, e.g. Customize/ Customise, Personalize/ Personalise.

 Click and drag on the title bar of a group to move the whole group

Naming groups

In their initial state, groups on the Start menu are either not named, or they have a default name, but it is possible to give them all their own individual names or titles. To do this:

1 Move the cursor over the top of a group and click on the current name or on this button at the right-hand side

Everyday apps ——

2 Double-click on the current name

Everyday apps

3 Enter a new name for the group

My best apps

4 The name is applied at the top of the group

Hot tip

Group names can be edited using the same process as when creating them in the first place.

Resizing Tiles

As well as rearranging tiles, their sizes can also be edited on the Start menu. Depending on the specific Windows app, there may be up to four options for resizing tiles in Windows 10: wide, large, medium and small, with the initial selection made for you:

1 Right-click on a tile to select it, and click on the **Resize** button from the context menu which appears

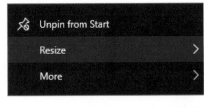

2 The current size of the tile is shown with a tick next to it

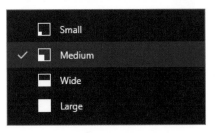

3 Click on another option to resize the tile

4 If the size is smaller, the tile is reduced in size and a gap appears around it (unless there is another tile small enough to fill the space next to it)

5 For a wide tile, there will be options for making it **Large**, **Medium** or **Small**

6 The **Large** size is the biggest available option for resizing tiles. Tiles that have been resized can be moved around the Start menu and other tiles will move automatically to accommodate them

7 Creating a range of different tile sizes is a good way to organize the Start menu and create a good mixture from a design point of view

Hot tip

The **Large** size is a good option for a tile that can then be used as a Live Tile, to display its contents or real-time information (see page 85).

The Desktop and Taskbar

After the use of the Start Screen in Windows 8 and 8.1, the Desktop is once again an integral part of Windows, and when you boot up Windows 10 it opens at the Desktop. This also displays the Taskbar at the bottom of the screen:

Hot tip

The Desktop can also be accessed by pressing **WinKey + D** or by right-clicking on the Start button and selecting **Desktop**.

Shortcut icons   Search box/Cortana   Desktop background

Start Button   Task View button   Taskbar

1   Move the cursor over items on the Taskbar to see open windows for that item. Click on a window to make that the active one

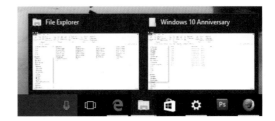

Don't forget

If an app has two or more windows open, each of them will be displayed when you move the cursor over the app's icon on the Taskbar.

2   The Notifications area at the right-hand side of the Taskbar has speaker, network and other system tools. Click on one to see more information about that item

Shutting Down

The method of shutting down in Windows 8 was another contentious issue, and one which has been addressed in Windows 10 by adding this functionality to the Start menu.

Shutting down from the Start menu

1 Click on the **Start** button

2 Click on the **Power** button

3 Click on either the **Sleep**, **Shut down** or **Restart** buttons; or

4 Right-click on the **Start** button and select either **Sign out**, **Sleep**, **Shut down** or **Restart** from the **Shut down or sign out** option

For some updates to Windows you will need to restart your computer for them to take effect.

Task View

A useful feature in Windows 10 is the Task View option. This is located on the Taskbar and can be used to view all open apps and also add new desktops. To use Task View:

 Click on this button on the Taskbar

 To show or hide the Task View button, right-click on the button and check On or Off the **Show Task View button** option

 The Task View displays minimized versions of the currently open apps and windows

Don't forget

Apps can only be open on one desktop at a time. So, if an app is open on one desktop and you try to open it on another, you will be taken to the desktop with the already open app. For adding additional desktops, see pages 36-37.

4 As more windows are opened, the format is arranged accordingly

 5 If an app has more than one window open, e.g. File Explorer, each window is displayed within Task View

Don't forget

Although the shortcuts and background are the same for each Desktop, the Taskbar will change depending on the open apps.

6 Click on a window in Task View to make it the active window

Adding Desktops

Another function within Task View is for creating additional desktops. This can be useful if you want to separate different categories of tasks on your computer. For instance, you may want to keep your open entertainment apps on a different desktop to your productivity ones. To create additional desktops:

 Click on the **Task View** button on the Taskbar

 The current desktop is displayed with the open windows

If you add too many desktops it may become confusing in terms of the content on each one.

 Click on the **New desktop** button

4 The new desktop is displayed at the bottom of the Task View window

5 Click on the new desktop to access it. Each desktop has the same background and shortcuts

The default names of different desktops cannot be changed, i.e. they are Desktop 1, Desktop 2, etc.

37

6 Open apps on the new desktop. These will be separate from the apps on any other desktop

To delete a desktop, click on the Task View button and click on the cross that appears when you hover your mouse over the desktop you want to remove.

7 Click on the **Task View** button to move between desktops

In the Anniversary Update, the Action Center groups together notifications from specific apps, so that it is easier to view them all and also remove them using the **Clear all** button in the top right-hand corner.

Click on a notification to open it and view its full contents.

Notifications for certain apps also appear onscreen for a short period of time in a small banner, to alert you to the fact that there is a new notification.

Notifications

In the modern digital world there is an increasing desire to keep updated about what is happening in our online world. With Windows 10, the Notifications panel (Action Center) can be used to display information from a variety of sources, so that you never miss an update or a notification from one of your apps. To view your notifications:

 Click on the **Notifications** button on the Taskbar. The counter denotes the number of new notifications

 New notifications appear at the top of the panel. For selecting what appears, see next page

ACTION CENTER — Clear all

Security and Maintenance

⚠ Verify your identity on this PC — Thu
Your saved credentials for apps, websites ⌄

Settings

⚙ Updates were installed — 3:28p

Collapse ⌄

Tablet mode	Connect	Note	All settings
Battery saver	VPN	Bluetooth	100%
PlusnetWireless s792287	Quiet hours	Location	Airplane mode

Ph... ∧ 12:08 PM 7/19/2015 ENG

3 Quick action buttons appear at the bottom of the panel. Click on an item to activate or deactivate it (when a button is blue, the item is active)

Settings for notifications

To change settings for the Notifications panel:

1 Click on the **Settings** app and access **System > Notifications & actions**

System
- Display
- Apps & features
- Default apps
- Notifications & actions

2 Under the **Quick actions** heading, click on the items and drag them into a new position to change where they appear in the Notifications panel

Quick actions

Press and hold (or select) quick actions, then drag to rearrange them. These quick actions appear in action center.

Tablet mode | Network | Note | All settings
Airplane mode | Location | Quiet hours | Brightness
Bluetooth | VPN | Battery saver | Project
Connect

Add or remove quick actions

3 Click on the **Add or remove quick actions** link to turn **On** or **Off** the default items on the Taskbar

Add or remove quick actions

- All settings — On
- Network — On
- Connect — On
- Project — On
- Battery saver — On

4 Under the **Get notifications from these senders** heading, drag the buttons **On** or **Off** to specify the items that appear in the Notifications panel. For instance, if the **Email and accounts** button (or the **Mail** button) is **On**, you will be notified whenever you receive a new email

Get notifications from these senders

Select a sender to see more settings. Some senders might also have their own notification settings. If so, open the sender to change them.

- AutoPlay — On
  On: Banners, Sounds
- Calendar — On
  On: Banners, Sounds
- Cortana — On
  On: Banners, Sounds

Hot tip

If notification icons are added to the Taskbar, their options can be selected by right-clicking on them.

NEW

Hot tip

Notifications can also be shown on the Lock Screen by dragging the **Show notifications on the lock screen** button to **On** in the **Notifications & actions** settings.

Show notifications on the lock screen
On

Personalization

Chapter 5 details a range of personalization options that can be applied from the Control Panel. Within the Personalization section of the Settings app there are also options to personalize the look of Windows 10. To do this:

 Open the **Settings** app and click on the **Personalization** button

Personalization
Background, lock screen, colors

 Click on the **Background** button to select a Desktop background. Select **Picture** in the Background box and click to select a picture or click on the **Browse** button to select one of your own pictures

Don't forget

In Windows 10, more of the personalization options have been moved into the Settings app. However, there are still some options within the Control panel, including Themes, Sounds and the Screen saver (under **Appearance and Personalization** > **Personalization**). See Chapter 5 for details.

40

 Click on the **Colors** button to select an accent color for the current background, Start menu and Taskbar

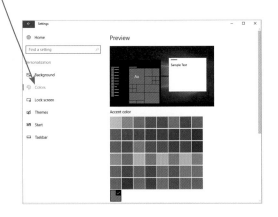

4 Check this box to **Off** to disable the automatic selection for the accent color

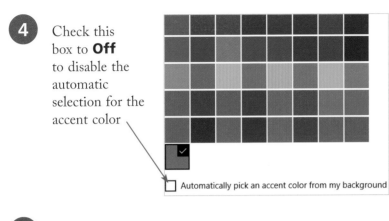

☐ Automatically pick an accent color from my background

5 Click on one of the colors to select it for the accent color

6 Drag this button **On** to make the Start menu, Taskbar and Action Center transparent

7 Drag this button **On** to use the color selected in Step 5 on the Start menu, Taskbar and Action Center

Make Start, taskbar, and action center transparent
● On

Show color on Start, taskbar, and action center
● On

8 Click on the **Themes** > **Theme settings** button to select a color theme for Windows 10, via the Control Panel

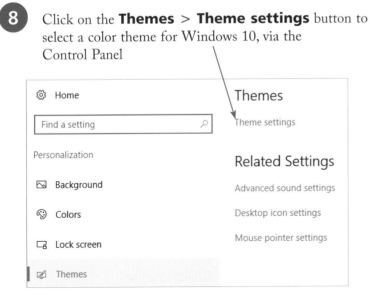

⚙ Home

Find a setting   𝒫

Personalization

🖼 Background

🎨 Colors

🖵 Lock screen

✍ Themes

Themes

Theme settings

Related Settings

Advanced sound settings

Desktop icon settings

Mouse pointer settings

Hot tip

For details about personalizing the Lock screen, see pages 42-43.

Lock Screen Settings

The Settings app enables you to set the appearance of the Lock screen, the Start menu and select an account photo. To do this, first access the Settings:

1 Open the **Settings** app and click on the **Personalization** button

More customization options can be applied using the Control Panel as in previous versions of Windows. For more information about this, see Chapter 5.

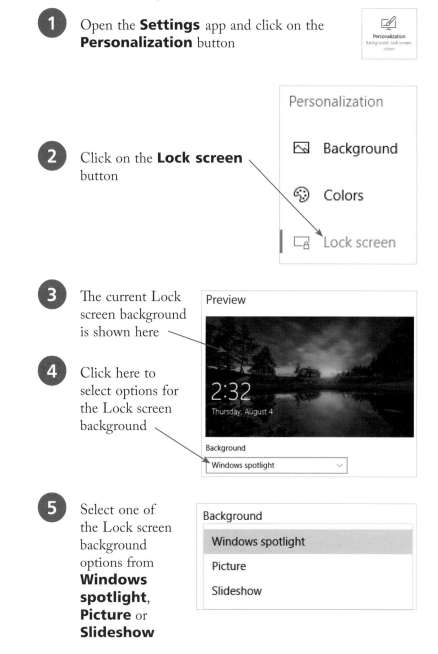

2 Click on the **Lock screen** button

3 The current Lock screen background is shown here

4 Click here to select options for the Lock screen background

5 Select one of the Lock screen background options from **Windows spotlight**, **Picture** or **Slideshow**

6 For the Picture option, click on the **Browse** button to select your own picture

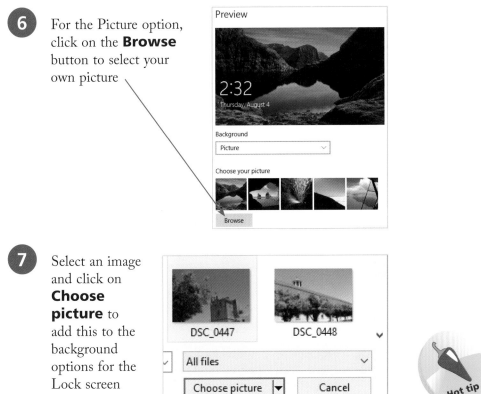

7 Select an image and click on **Choose picture** to add this to the background options for the Lock screen

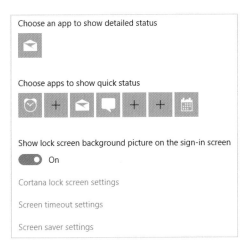

8 Other options for the Lock screen include selecting apps that display their detailed or quick status, options for screen timeout when not in use, and Screen saver settings

Hot tip

If you use your own images for the Lock screen background, these will remain available on the thumbnail row even if you switch to another image for the background.

43

Settings

Accessing Settings

The Settings in Windows 10 provide options for how you set up your computer and how it operates. There are nine main categories of Settings, each of which have a number of sub-categories. The Settings app can be accessed in a number of ways:

1 Click on the **Start** button

2 Click on the **Settings** button on the Start menu or the **Settings** tile on the Start menu; or

3 Click on the **Notifications** button on the Taskbar

4 Click on the **All settings** button; or

5 Enter **Settings** into the **Search** box and click on the **Settings** button

6 In the **Settings** app, click on one of the main categories to view the options within that category

Add the Settings app to the Taskbar for quick access. To do this, access it from the Start menu, right-click on it and click on **More** > **Pin to taskbar**.

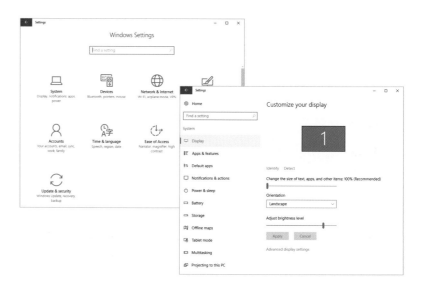

System Settings

The System Settings provide numerous options to specify how your computer looks and operates. They include:

- **Display**. This contains options for changing the size of items on the screen, the orientation of the screen, and options for adjusting the screen brightness, either manually or automatically.

- **Apps & features**. This contains information about the apps that you have on your computer. This includes their size and installation date. Click on an app and click on the **Uninstall** button to remove it.

Apps can also be uninstalled from within the Control Panel (**Programs > Uninstall a program**).

45

- **Default apps**. This can be used to select default apps for opening certain items, such as music, photos and videos. It can also be used to specify a default email app.

- **Notifications & actions**. This contains options for selecting which notification icons appear on the Taskbar, and specifying which apps can be used to display notifications, e.g. your calendar and email.

- **Power & sleep**. This contains options for when the screen is turned off when not being used, and when the computer goes to sleep when it is not being used. This ranges from one minute to never.

- **Battery**. This can be used on laptops, and displays the charge level of the battery and what is using the battery most. It also has options for saving battery power.

...cont'd

- **Storage**. This displays how much storage has been taken up on your computer and has options for where you want to save certain types of content. This can be the PC or an external drive, such as a hard drive or a USB flash drive.

- **Offline maps**. This contains options for downloading maps so that you can use them even when you are offline. There is also an option for only downloading maps when you are connected to Wi-Fi, to save any unwanted charges if you have a mobile data plan.

- **Tablet mode**. This can be used on desktop and laptop computers, using a mouse and keyboard to replicate the operation of using a touchscreen device or tablet with Windows 10. This includes expanding the Start menu to full screen.

- **Multitasking**. This contains options for working with windows and desktops. In the **Snap** section you can turn on options for arranging windows when they are moved to the edge of the screen, and in the **Virtual desktops** section you can specify whether the Taskbar (and Alt + Tab) shows all open windows, or just those for the current desktop.

- **Projecting to this PC**. This can be used to allow other Windows 10 devices (computers, tablets or phones) to project their screens on to your computer so that you can view the screen and also interact with it.

- **Apps for websites**. This can be used to allow compatible apps to open websites, rather than using a browser.

- **About**. This contains information about your computer and the version of Windows that you are using.

Devices Settings

The Devices Settings provide settings for how the hardware connected with your computer operates. They include:

- **Printers & scanners**. This can be used to add new printers or scanners to your computer. These can either be wireless ones, or ones which connect via cable. In most cases, the required software will be installed with Windows 10, or if not, it will be downloaded from the internet.

- **Connected devices**. This can be used to add new devices, such as a printer, using the **Add a device** button.

- **Bluetooth**. This can be used to link your computer to compatible Bluetooth devices, so that they can share content over short distances with radiowaves. The two devices have to be 'paired' initially to be able to share content.

- **Mouse & touchpad**. This contains options for customizing the mouse and touchpad (for a laptop). These include setting the main button on the mouse (Left by default) and how the scrolling operates with the mouse, such as the number of lines that can be scrolled at a time (Multiple by default).

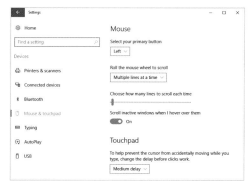

- **Typing**. This contains options for correcting your typing as you go. These include autocorrecting misspelt words, and highlighting misspelt words.

- **AutoPlay**. This contains options for applying AutoPlay for external devices such as removable drives and memory cards. If AutoPlay is On, the devices will be activated and accessed when they are attached to your computer.

- **USB**. This can be used to flag up any issues with connected USB devices.

Printers can also be added through the **Control Panel**. This is done in the **Devices and Printers** section, under **Hardware and Sound**. Click on the **Add a printer** button and follow the wizard.

47

...cont'd

Network & Internet Settings

The Network & Internet Settings provide settings related to connecting to networks, usually for accessing the internet. They include:

If Wi-Fi is turned **On** in the Wi-Fi settings, any routers in range should be recognized. A password will probably then be required to connect to the router.

- **Status**. This displays the current Wi-Fi status, i.e. whether the computer is connected to the internet or not.

- **Wi-Fi**. This contains options for connecting to the internet via your Wi-Fi router (or public hotspots). There is also an option for managing your Wi-Fi networks.

- **Ethernet**. This can be used if you are connecting to the internet with an Ethernet cable. This connects to the Ethernet port on your computer and internet access is delivered through the use of your telephone line.

- **Dial-up**. This can be used if you have a dial-up modem for connecting to the internet. This is not common these days but is still a valid means of internet access.

- **VPN**. This can be used to connect to a corporate network over VPN (Virtual Private Network). If you are doing this you will need certain settings and details from your network administrator.

- **Airplane mode**. This can be used to turn off wireless communication when you are on a plane, so that you can still use your computer (laptop) safely.

- **Mobile hotspot**. This can be used to determine how the computer interacts with mobile hotspots for connecting to shared public networks.

- **Data usage**. This displays how much data has been downloaded over any networks that you are using. The most common one is Wi-Fi and displays your usage over a 30 day period.

- **Proxy**. This contains options for using a proxy server for Ethernet or Wi-Fi connections.

48

Personalization Settings

The Personalization Settings provide options for customizing the look and feel of Windows 10. They include:

- **Background**. This can be used to change the Desktop background in Windows 10. You can select images from the pictures provided, solid colors, a slideshow or your own photos (using the **Browse** button). You can also choose how the background fits the screen (the default is Fill).

- **Colors**. This contains options for selecting a color for borders, buttons, the Taskbar and the Start menu background.

- **Lock screen**. This can be used to select a background for the Lock screen. You can use the images provided and also select your own photos (using the **Browse** button). You can also select apps that display relevant information on the Lock screen, such as email notifications or calendar events.

Hot tip

In the Colors section there is also an option for making the Start menu, Taskbar and Action Center (Notifications) transparent. This is accessed beneath the color chart for selecting an accent color.

49

Settings

⚙ Home

Find a setting

Personalization

🖼 Background

🎨 Colors

🔲 Lock screen

🖌 Themes

🗖 Start

🖵 Taskbar

Preview

10:14
Friday, August 5

Background

Picture

Choose your picture

Browse

- **Themes**. This contains a link to the Control Panel, where color themes can be applied for several elements within the Windows 10 interface.

- **Start**. This contains options for how the Start menu operates. It can be used to view the Start menu in full screen mode and also display recently used items in the Start menu.

- **Taskbar**. This contains options for locking the Taskbar, automatically hiding it, changing the icon size and specifying its screen location (left, top, right or bottom).

...cont'd

Accounts Settings

The Accounts Settings provide options for adding new online accounts (such as a new email account, or an online storage and sharing service such as Dropbox). They include:

- **Your info**.
  This displays information about your current account, which will either be the one you signed into using your Microsoft Account details, or a Local account, which has no online presence.
  You can also swap between accounts here.

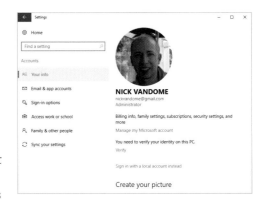

- **Email & app accounts**. This can be used to add email accounts and also add a Microsoft Account.

- **Sign-in options**. This contains security options for signing in to your account. You can create a PIN, Password or Picture password. Whichever method you choose, this will be required when you sign in to your account from the Lock screen.

- **Access work or school**. This can be used to connect to a workplace network, where you can share certain items. To do this you will need to contact the network administrator in order to obtain the correct settings to connect to the network.

- **Family & other people**. This can be used to set up accounts on your computer for other family members, or friends. They will be able to set their own sign-in options and you will be able to switch users by clicking on the Start button and then clicking on the icon of the current user.

- **Sync your settings**. This can be used to sync the settings you have on your computer with any other Windows 10 devices that you have. For instance, if you have a desktop computer using Windows 10 you will be able to sync settings and apps with another Windows 10 device, such as a Surface tablet.

The Accounts Settings can be used to switch between a Microsoft Account and a Local account for signing in to your PC.

...cont'd

Time & Language Settings

The Time & Language Settings provide options for the time zone used by your computer and the format for these items. They include:

● **Date & time**. This can be used to set the date and time, either manually, or automatically, using the **Time zone** drop-down menu. There is also a link to **Related settings** in the Control Panel, where formatting options can be applied.

The date and time can be set within the **Clock, Language, and Region** section of the Control Panel, under the **Date and Time** heading.

51

● **Region & language**. This can be used to select the language that is used by your computer, e.g. English (United States). You can also add new languages.

● **Speech**. This contains options for how the speech function operates when using Windows 10. This includes the language to use when you are using speech, and also the default voice if using apps that speak text from the screen.

...cont'd

Ease of Access Settings

The Ease of Access Settings contain a range of options to help users who have visual or motor issues when using a computer. They include:

- **Narrator**. This can be used to activate a screen reader so text, buttons and toolbars can be read out loud. You can choose a voice style for the narrator and the speed and pitch of reading.

- **Magnifier**. This can be used to magnify what is being viewed on the screen. The amount of magnification can be increased by up to 1600% of the standard view. The color of the screen can also be inverted.

- **High contrast**. This contains options for applying high contrast themes for Windows 10, to make certain elements more pronounced. This can be useful for users with dyslexia.

- **Closed captions**. This can be used by hearing-impaired users to provide text subtitles for items such as movies or multimedia content. The captioning is included in the media and the settings enable you to select color, size and effects for the subtitles.

- **Keyboard**. This can be used to enable the on-screen keyboard and options for keyboard shortcuts and keyboard sounds for when certain keys are pressed, e.g. Caps Lock and Number Lock.

- **Mouse**. This contains options for setting the size of the mouse pointer and also its color.

- **Other options**. This contains options for turning Off animations and Windows backgrounds, to make the screen less distracting, and also options for showing notifications.

Privacy Settings

The Privacy Settings can be used to allow or deny certain apps access to your location. This can make them operate more efficiently, but you may not want all of your apps to function in this way. They include:

- **General**. This contains options for allowing or denying apps access to some of your personal information (such as name, picture and account info), using a SmartScreen Filter to check web pages used by certain apps, send Microsoft information about your typing, and allowing websites to provide you with local information based on your default language being used.

- **Location**. This can be used to turn On or Off the location services, to allow or deny apps the use of your current location.

- **Notifications**. This can be used to specify which apps can be used to show notifications in the Action Center and also on the Lock screen.

- The following options can be used to allow or deny apps access to these specific functions: **Camera**, **Microphone**, **Contacts**, **Calendar**, **Call history**, **Messaging** and **Radios**.

- **Speech, inking & typing**. This can be used to train Windows and the Personal Digital Assistant, Cortana, to your writing and speaking styles, so that they can operate more efficiently.

- **Account info**. This can be used to allow apps access to your name, picture and account info.

- **Email**. This can be used to specify which apps can access email, e.g. the People app for using Contacts.

- **Other devices**. This can be used to view external devices, such as an Xbox, which have access to your apps.

- **Feedback & diagnostics**. This contains options for how feedback is requested by Microsoft. It can be set to automatically, or for a specific time period, e.g. once a week.

- **Background apps**. This can be used to specify which apps can receive notifications and updates even when not in use. This includes Mail and the Microsoft Edge browser.

Beware

The more access you give in terms of your own information and allowing apps to share your location, the more unwanted information you may be sent.

...cont'd

Update & security

The Update & security Settings provide options for installing updates to Windows and also backing up and recovering the data on your computer. They include:

- **Windows Update**. This can be used to install system updates, such as those to Windows 10 and also important security updates. They can be set to be checked for and installed automatically (using the **Advanced options** button) or manually using the **Check for updates** button. For some updates, your computer will shut down and restart automatically.

Because of the nature of Windows 10, e.g. it is designed as an online service, there will be regular updates. Check the Windows Update section regularly, even if you have set updates to be installed automatically, as you will be able to view the details of installed updates.

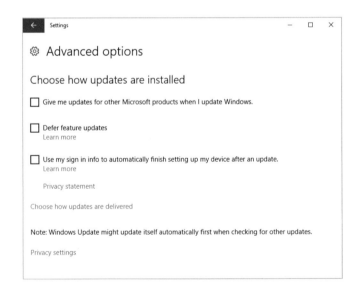

- **Windows Defender**. This contains options for protecting your computer with the Windows Defender app, including real-time protection and also Cloud protection for items that are stored online, such as in OneDrive.

- **Backup**. This can be used to back up your important files and documents. It is best if this is done to an external hard drive that is kept separately from your computer. Connect an external hard drive and click on the **Add a back-up location on this PC** button to start the process.

- **Recovery**. This can be used if you encounter problems with the way that Windows 10 is operating. You can select to refresh your computer and keep all of your files intact (although they should always be backed up first); reinstall Windows completely, which will reset it completely and you will lose all of your files and any apps you have downloaded; or return to an earlier version of Windows that was on your computer, without losing any files.

- **Activation**. This can be used to activate your copy of Windows 10, to confirm that it is an authorized version. Activation can be done online.

- **Find My Device**. This can be used to set up Find My Device for locating a lost device, via the website at: **account.microsoft.com/devices**

- **For developers**. This contains options for advanced users involved in programming and app development.

- **Windows Insider Program**. This can be used to gain access to the Insider Program, for downloading preview versions of the latest Windows 10 updates.

Searching

Searching for items and information on computers and the internet has come a long way since the first search engines on the web. Most computer operating systems now have sophisticated search facilities for finding things on your own computer as well as searching over the web. They also now have Personal Digital Assistants, which are voice activated search functions, which can be used instead of typing search requests.

Windows 10 has a search box built-in to the Taskbar, which also includes the Personal Digital Assistant, Cortana. This can also be used for a wide range of voice activated tasks.

Using the Search box for text searching
To use the Search box for text-only searches, over either your computer or the web:

1 Click in the Search box

2 Enter a search term (or website address)

3 Click on one of the results, or on the **Search the web** button, to view the search results page in the Microsoft Edge browser

The top search result is displayed at the top of the window in Step 2.

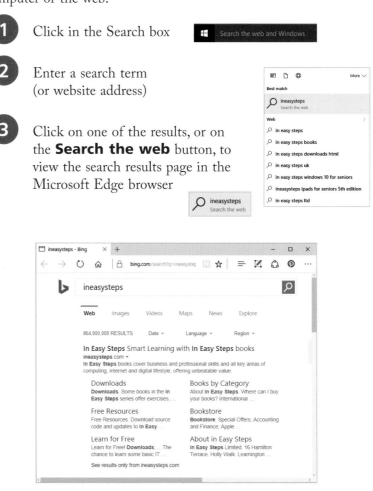

Asking a question

The Search box can also be used to ask specific questions:

 1 Enter a question in the Search box

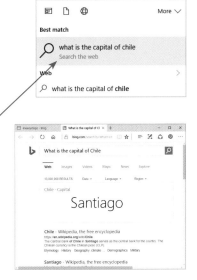

 2 Click on the **Search the web** button at the top of the Search box to view the results in the Microsoft Edge browser (in some instances, the answer will be displayed at the top of the Cortana Search box too)

The magnifying glass icon indicates that a search is going to be undertaken on the web and this will be displayed on a search results page, as in Step 2.

Searching over your computer

As well as searching over the web, the Search box can also be used to find items on your computer:

 1 Enter a search query into the Search box and click on one of the results to open the item on your computer

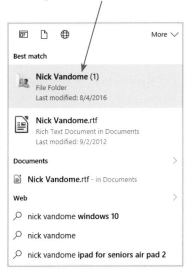

If you are searching for a keyword over files on your computer, the search will be conducted over the text in documents and folders, not just the document titles. It will also search over the online backup and storage facility, OneDrive, if you have this set up.

Setting Up Cortana

To ensure that you can use Cortana to perform voice searches and queries, the language settings on your Windows 10 computer have to be set up correctly. To do this:

1 Open the **Settings** app and click on the **Time & language** button

2 Click on the **Region & language** button

3 Click here to select a country or region

Country or region

Windows and apps might use your country or region to give you local content

United Kingdom

Languages

You can type in any language you add to the list. Windows, apps and websites will appear in the first language in the list that they support

+ Add a language

English (United States)
Windows display language

English (United Kingdom)
Language pack installed

Set as default | Options | Remove

Don't forget

The county or region, display language and speech language should be the same in order for Cortana to work.

4 Click on the required display language and click on the **Set as default** button

5 Click on the **Speech** button under **Time & language**

🎤 Speech

6 Select the same **Speech language** as the one used as the display language in Step 4

Hot tip

If the Cortana Search box is not displayed once the languages have been set, restart your computer to apply the changes.

Speech language

Choose the language you speak with your device

English (United Kingdom) ∨

Using Cortana

Once the correct languages have been selected for Cortana, you have to ensure that your computer's microphone is working properly since it will be used for voice queries with Cortana.

Setting up the microphone
To set up your computer's microphone:

1 Open the **Settings** app and click on the **Time & language** button

Time & language
Speech, region, date

2 Click on the **Speech** button

🎤 Speech

3 Under the **Microphone** section, click on the **Get started** button

Microphone

Set up your mic for speech recognition

Get started

4 In the microphone wizard, click on the **Next** button

← 🎤 Set up your mic   ✕

Microphone (Realtek High Definition Audio)

I'll give you a phrase to repeat so I can make sure I'm hearing you correctly. Make sure you're in a quiet place, and your microphone is set up correctly.

Next   Cancel

5 Repeat the phrase in the wizard window to complete setting up your microphone. (If the setup is successful, the wizard will move to the completion page automatically)

← 🎤 Set up your mic   ✕

Read the following sentences to complete setting up the microphone:

"Peter talks to his computer. He prefers it to typing, and particularly prefers it to pen and paper."

Next   Cancel

6 Click on the **Finish** button

Finish

Beware

Most modern laptop computers have built-in microphones, but an external one may need to be attached to a desktop computer.

Beware

It can take Cortana a bit of time to fully recognize your voice and style of speech. Make sure that there is no loud background noise when you are using Cortana.

...cont'd

Searching with Cortana

As with text searches, Cortana can be used to search over various places and for different items:

 Click on the microphone button in the Search box to begin a voice search

 The Cortana symbol is displayed in the Search window with the word **Listening...** in the Search box. Say what you want to find

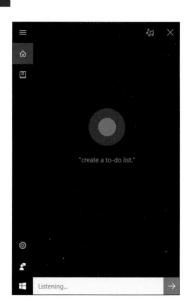

 If Cortana cannot understand what you said, you are asked to try again

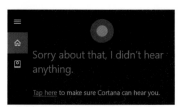

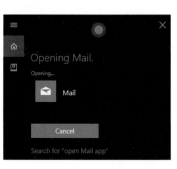 Cortana can be used to open specific apps, e.g. by saying **Open Mail**

Hot tip

In the Anniversary Update, Cortana can be used directly from the Lock screen, to ask general queries, such as 'What is the weather in my area?' or to play a song from the Groove Music app.

5 If the query is general, e.g. **Open Microsoft**, various options will be displayed

6 For a specific request, e.g. **Open Microsoft Edge**, the required app will be opened

Cortana Settings

Settings for Cortana can be accessed from the Search window:

1 Click on the **Settings** button on the sidebar

2 Apply the Cortana Settings as required, including an option for Cortana to provide its own suggestions, and also setting Cortana to respond to saying **Hey Cortana** from any screen or app

3 Scroll up the Settings window to access more options

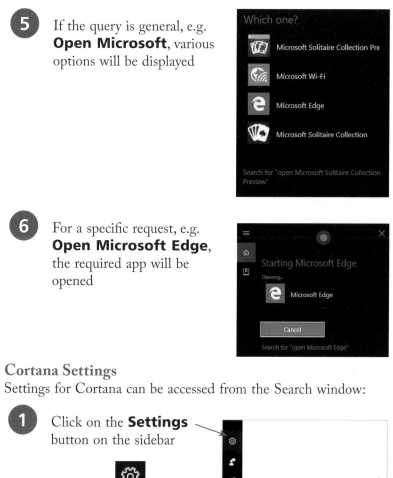

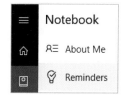

Hot tip

The Notebook within Cortana can also be used to specify settings for a range of topics that are monitored by Cortana. These include items such as Eat & Drink, Events, Finance, News, Sports and Travel. If the options are turned **On** you will automatically receive notifications and recommendations for these subjects.

Setting Reminders

The Cortana Search box can also be used to set reminders that appear when required. To do this:

1 Click in the Search box and click on this button on the side toolbar

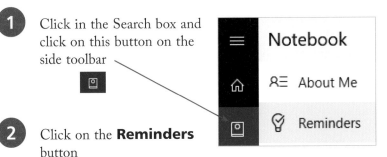

2 Click on the **Reminders** button

3 Click on this button to add a new reminder

4 Click in the **Remember to...** text box to add the item for which you want the reminder

5 Enter the reminder item details

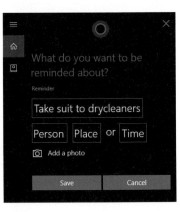

Hot tip

If the Person or Place option is selected for a reminder, a specific person can be selected from your contacts in the People app, or a geographic location. These can also be used in conjunction with a specific time.

6 Click in the **Time** text box to set a time for the reminder

7 Select a time for the reminder by clicking on the required item. Click on the **Another time...** button to set a custom time for the reminder

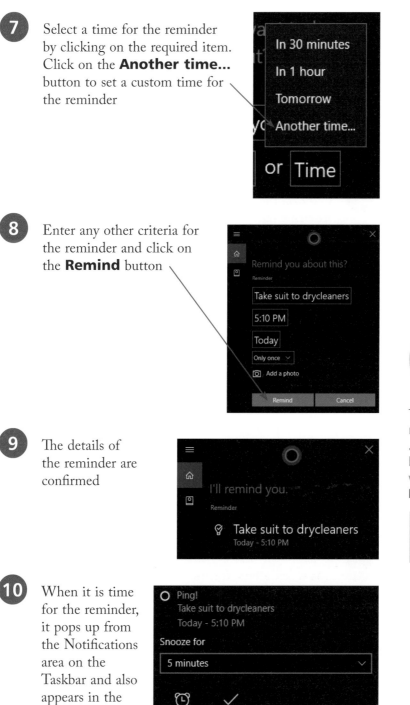

8 Enter any other criteria for the reminder and click on the **Remind** button

9 The details of the reminder are confirmed

10 When it is time for the reminder, it pops up from the Notifications area on the Taskbar and also appears in the Cortana window

Don't forget

To view completed reminders, click on the **...** menu button at the bottom of the reminders window and click on the **History** button.

Adding and Switching Users

If more than one person uses the computer, each person can have a user account defined with a username and a password. To create a new user account, as either a Microsoft Account or a Local account:

 Access the **Settings** app and select **Accounts**

Accounts
Your accounts, email, sync, work, family

 Click on the **Family & other people** button

Accounts

ᴀ≡ Your info

✉ Email & app accounts

🔍 Sign-in options

💼 Access work or school

🧑₊ Family & other people

Beware

The email address is a required field when creating a new user with a Microsoft Account.

 Click on the **Add a family member** button

Your family

You can allow family members to sign in to this PC. Adults can manage family settings online and see recent activity to help kids stay safe.

➕ Add a family member

4 Select whether the account is for a child or an adult. For a child, this provides online security options

Add an adult or a child?

Enter the email address of the person you want to invite. If they use Xbox Live, Outlook.com, Windows, or OneDrive, enter the email address they use to login.

🔘 Add a child
Kids are safer online when they have their own account

⚪ Add an adult

[Email address]

The person I want to invite doesn't have an email address

5 Enter the name of the new user, an email address and a password to create a Microsoft Account for the user

Let's create an account

Windows, Office, Outlook.com, OneDrive, Skype, Xbox. They're all better and more personal when you sign in with your Microsoft account. Learn more

Lucy	Vandome

✔ After you sign up, we'll send you a message with a link to verify this user name.

lucyvandome@gmail.com
Get a new email address

••••••••

United Kingdom

Back   Next

6 Click on the **Next** button to complete the setup wizard

Next

7 The user is added to the Accounts pages

Other users

Allow people who are not part of your family to sign in with their own accounts. This won't add them to your family.

➕ Add someone else to this PC

👤 lucyvandome@gmail.com

8 Click on a user to change the type of their account, e.g. from a Local account to a Microsoft Account, or to delete their account

👤 lucyvandome@gmail.com

Change account type   Remove

Hot tip

Family Safety settings can be applied by clicking on the **Manage family settings online** link on the **Family & other people** page. This takes you to your online Microsoft Account page where settings can be applied for items such as web filtering, time controls and app restrictions.

...cont'd

Switching users

If you have a number of user accounts defined on the computer (several accounts can be active at the same time), you do not need to close your apps and log off to be able to switch to another user. It is easy to switch back and forth.

When switching users, all of your settings and files are maintained but the new user will not be able to see them, and you will not be able to see theirs when you switch back. Your screen should look exactly the same as you left it.

 Click on the **Start** button

 Click on another user's name. They will have to enter their own password in order to access their account, at which point they will be signed in. You can then switch between users without each having to log out each time

As an alternative way to switch users:

 Press **WinKey** + **L** to lock the current user

Access the Log on screen for all of the current users and select one as required

Shut down

When you turn off your computer (see page 33), you will be warned if there are other user accounts still logged on to the computer.

If the other accounts have data files open, shutting down without logging them off could cause them to lose information.

Click on the **Shut down anyway** button to shut down without other users logging off

Someone else is still using this PC. If you shut down now, they could lose unsaved work.

Shut down anyway

3 Working with Apps

"Apps" is one of the new buzzwords in computing. Put simply, it is just another name for computer programs. In Windows 10, some apps are pre-installed, as with previous versions of Windows, while hundreds more can be downloaded from the Windows Store. This chapter shows how to work with and organize apps in Windows 10, and how to find your way around the Windows Store.

Starting with Apps

The word "app" may be seen by some as a new-fangled piece of techno-speak. But, simply, it means a computer program. Originally, apps were items that were downloaded to smartphones and tablet computers. However, the terminology has now been expanded to cover any computer program. So, in Windows 10 most programs are referred to as "apps", although some legacy ones may still be referred to as "programs".

There are three clear types of apps within Windows 10:

- **Windows 10 apps**. These are the built-in apps that can be accessed from the Start menu. They cover the areas of communication, entertainment and information and several of them are linked together through the online sharing service, OneDrive. In Windows 10 they open in their own window on the Desktop, in the same way as the older-style Windows apps (see below).

- **Windows classic apps**. These are the older-style Windows apps that people may be familiar with from previous versions of Windows. These open in the Desktop environment.

- **Windows Store apps**. These are apps that can be downloaded from the online Windows Store, and cover a wide range of subjects and functionality. Some Windows Store apps are free, while others have to be paid for.

Windows 10 apps

Windows 10 apps are accessed from the brightly-colored tiles on the Start menu (or listed on the left-hand side). Click on a tile to open the relevant app:

In Windows 10 all apps open directly on the Desktop and their operation is more consistent, regardless of the type of app.

Windows classic apps

The Windows classic apps are generally the ones that appeared as default with previous versions of Windows, and would have been accessed from the Start button. The Windows classic apps can be accessed from the Start menu by using the alphabetic list, or searched for via the Taskbar Search box. Windows classic apps have the traditional Windows look and functionality, and they also open on the Desktop.

Some older Windows apps, such as Notepad and Paint, can be found in the Windows Accessories folder in the All Apps list. Alternatively, they can be searched for using the Cortana Search box.

Windows Store apps

The Windows Store apps are accessed and downloaded from the online Windows Store. Apps can be browsed and searched for in the Store, and when they are downloaded they are added to the All apps section of the Start menu.

The Windows Store is accessed by clicking on the **Store** tile on the Start menu or on the Taskbar.

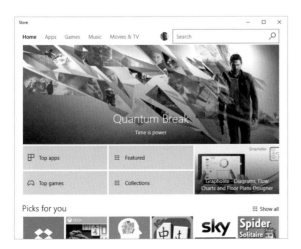

Windows 10 Apps

The Windows 10 apps that are accessed from the All apps list on the Start menu cover a range of communication, entertainment and information functions. The apps include:

 Alarms & Clock. This provides alarms, clocks for times around the world, a timer and a stopwatch function.

 Calculator. This is a standard calculator that also has an option for using it as a scientific calculator.

 Calendar. This is a calendar which you can use to add appointments and important dates.

 Camera. This can be used to take photos directly onto your computer, but only if it has a built in camera.

 Connect. This can be used to connect a PC so that it can be used as a wireless projector.

 Cortana. This is the Personal Digital Assistant for Windows 10 that can be used to search for a variety of items.

 Groove Music. This can be used to access the online Music Store where music can be downloaded.

 Mail. This is the online Mail facility. You can use it to connect to a selection of email accounts.

 Maps. This provides online access to maps from around the world. It also shows traffic issues.

 Messaging. This can be used to send text messages to other users, using a Microsoft Account.

 Microsoft Edge. This is the new default browser in Windows 10, replacing Internet Explorer.

 Money. This is one of the information apps that provides real-time financial news. This is based on your location as entered when you installed Windows 10.

 Movies & TV. This is where you'll see the movies and TV shows you buy in the Windows Store, and also your personal videos. There is also a link to the Video Store.

See Chapter 9 for more information about working with the Microsoft Edge browser.

See Chapter 10 for more information about working with the Calendar, Mail, People and Skype apps, and how content can be shared between the different apps.

News. This is one of the information apps that provides real-time news information. This is based on your location as entered at installation.

 OneDrive. This is an online facility for storing and sharing content from your computer. This includes photos and documents.

 OneNote. This is the Microsoft note-taking app, part of the Office suite of apps.

 People. This is the address book app for adding contacts. Your contacts from sites such as Facebook and Twitter can also be imported into the People app.

 Photos. This can be used to view and organize your photos. You can also share and print photos directly from the Photos app.

 Reader. This can be used to open and view documents in different file formats, such as PDF and TIFF.

 Settings. This can be used to access all of the main settings for customizing and managing Windows 10 and your computer. (See pages 44-55 for details.)

 Sport. This is one of the information apps that provides real-time sports news. This is based on your location as entered when you installed Windows 10.

 Sticky Notes. This is an app for creating short notes that can be 'stuck' to the screen, so that they are readily visible.

 Store. This provides access to the online Windows Store from where a range of other apps can be bought and downloaded to your computer.

 Weather. This provides real-time weather forecasts for locations around the world. By default it will provide the nearest forecast to your location as entered when you installed Windows 10.

 Xbox. This can be used to download and play games, and also play online Xbox games.

OneDrive can also be used to share your content, such as photos and documents, with other people. See pages 160-163 for details.

The information in the Money, News, Sports and Weather apps is provided by Bing.

71

Using Windows 10 Apps

In Windows 8 and 8.1, the newer style Windows apps had a different look and functionality. However, in Windows 10 all of the apps have been created with a more consistent appearance, although there are still some differences.

Windows 10 apps

Windows 10 apps now open in their own window on the Desktop (in Windows 8 and 8.1 they only opened in full screen) and they can be moved and resized in the same way as older-style apps:

1 Click and drag on the top toolbar to move the app's window

In Windows 10 there has been a conscious effort to achieve a greater consistency between the newer style apps and the old, classic style apps.

2 Drag on the bottom or right-hand border to resize the app's window (or the bottom right-hand corner to resize the height and width simultaneously)

Windows 10 app menus

Some Windows 10 apps have their own menus:

1 Click on this button (if available) within the app's window to access its menu

Groove Music

Groove Music

Search

🎧 Your Groove

◎ Albums

👤 Artists

2 Click on the menu button again to minimize the menu to just the icons, without text

Don't forget

Apps that are installed from a CD or DVD are automatically included on the alphabetical list on the Start menu.

73

3 Click this button to move to previously viewed pages within the app

← Groove Music

≡ Albums

Managing an app's window

As with older-style apps, the Windows 10 apps also have the same control buttons on the top toolbar:

— ☐ ✕

1 Click on this button to close the app

✕

2 Click on this button to maximize the app's window

☐

3 Click on this button to minimize the app's window (it will be minimized onto the Taskbar)

—

Classic Apps on the Desktop

The Windows classic apps open on the Desktop, in the same way as with previous versions of Windows, even though they are opened from the Start menu (or the Taskbar).

Opening a Windows system app

To open a Windows system app:

 Click on the **Start** button and navigate through the app list

 Select the app you want to open

 The app opens on the Desktop

Hot tip

If apps have been pinned to the Taskbar, as shown on page 79, they can be opened directly from there by simply clicking on them.

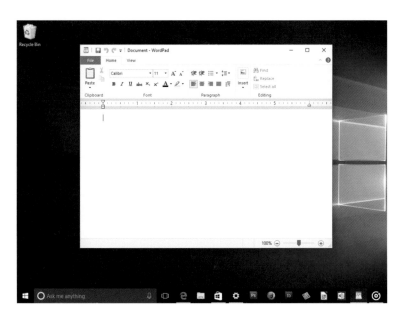

 Click on the tabs at the top of the app to access relevant Ribbon toolbars and menus

Closing Apps

There are several ways to close a Windows app:

 Click on the red **Close** button in the top right of the window

 Select **File** > **Exit** from the File menu (if available)

 Press **Alt** + **F4**

Beware

It is always worth saving a new document as soon as it is created. It should also be saved at regular intervals as you are working on it.

 Right-click on the icon on the Taskbar and select **Close window**

 If any changes have been made to the document, you may receive a warning message advising you to save the associated file

---

WordPad   ✕

Do you want to save changes to Document?

[Save]   [Don't Save]   [Cancel]

Viewing All Apps

There is a lot more to Windows 10 than the default Windows 10 apps. Most of the Windows apps that were available with previous versions of Windows are still there, and in the Windows 10 Anniversary Update they are all available directly from the Start button, on the Start menu. To access all of the apps:

1 Click on the **Start** button

The alphabetical list of apps in Step 2 replaces the **All Apps** button that was available in previous versions of Windows 10.

2 All of the apps are displayed. Use the scroll bar to move through all of the apps, which are listed alphabetically

3 Click on a letter heading to view an alphabetic grid for finding apps. Click on a letter to move to that section

Searching for Apps

As you acquire more and more apps, it may become harder to find the ones you want. To help with this, you can use the Search box to search over all of the apps on your computer. To do this:

1 Click in the Search box on the Taskbar

2 Enter a word in the Search box

3 As you type, relevant apps are displayed. When the one you are seeking appears, click on it to start the app

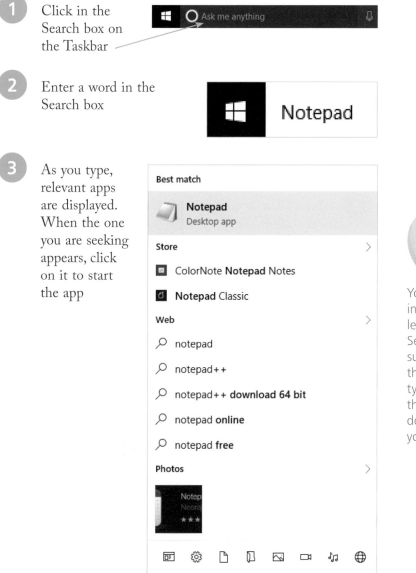

You just have to put in the first couple of letters of an app and Search will automatically suggest results based on this. The more that you type, the more specific the results become. Case does not matter when you are typing a search.

Pin to Start Menu

In most cases, you will want to have quick access to a variety of apps on the Start menu, not just the new Windows 10 apps. It is possible to "pin" any app to the Start menu so that it is always readily available. To do this:

 Access the alphabetical list of apps, from the Start button

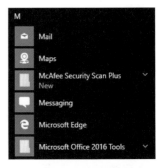

Right-click on an app and click on the **Pin to Start** button

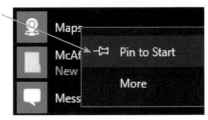

The app is pinned to the Start menu. It can now be repositioned, if required, as with any other app (see page 28)

78

Pin to Taskbar

All Windows 10 apps can be pinned to the Desktop Taskbar (the bar that appears along the bottom of the Desktop), so that they can be accessed quickly. To do this:

 Click on the **Start** button to access the full list of apps

 Right-click on an app and click on **More > Pin to taskbar**

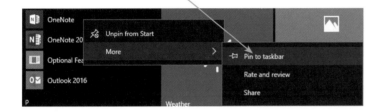

Hot tip

Apps can be unpinned from the Taskbar by right-clicking on them and selecting **More > Unpin from taskbar** from the contextual menu that appears.

The app is added to the Taskbar

Open apps on the Taskbar can also be pinned there by right-clicking on them and selecting **Pin to taskbar**

Pinned items remain on the Taskbar even once they have been closed

Using the Windows Store

The third category of apps that can be used with Windows 10 are those that are downloaded from the Windows Store. These cover a wide range of topics and they provide an excellent way to add functionality to Windows 10. To use the Windows Store:

Windows 10 apps can all be downloaded from the Windows Store.

1   Click on the **Store** tile on the Start menu

2   The currently featured apps are displayed on the Home screen

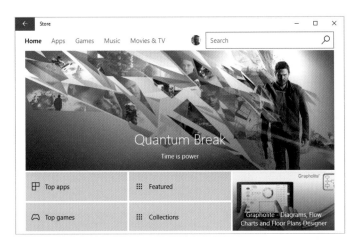

The Windows Store interface has been redesigned for the Anniversary Update to make it easier to find the apps that you want.

3   Scroll up and down to see additional featured apps

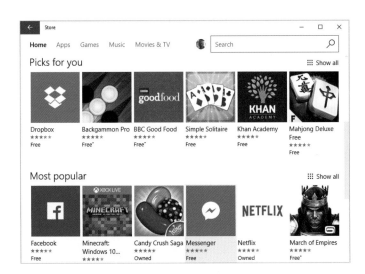

4 Click on the **Top apps** button on the Homepage and select apps under specific headings, e.g. **Best-rated** apps

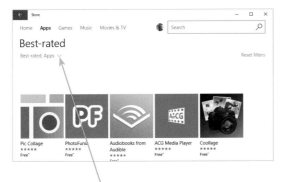

 5 Click here to select options for viewing apps according to certain criteria, e.g. **Top free**

6 Click on an app to preview it, and for more details

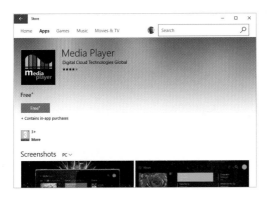

Scroll up and down in Step 6 to view ratings and reviews about the app and also any additional descriptions.

...cont'd

7 Click here to access the categories for a specific item, e.g. Top free apps

8 Click on a category to access it

9 Click on items in each category to view details about them. Click on the Back arrow to go back up one level each time

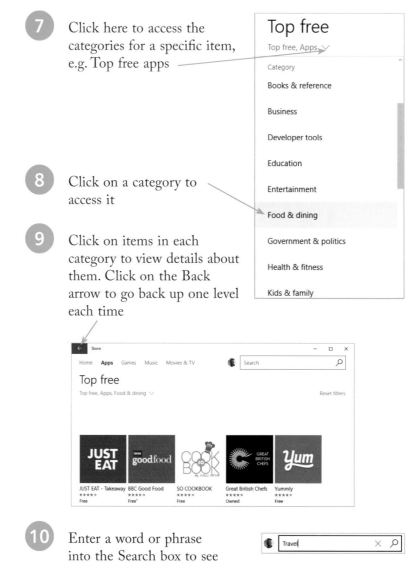

Hot tip

To return to the Home screen at any point, click on the **Home** button from the top toolbar.

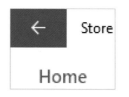

10 Enter a word or phrase into the Search box to see matching apps. Click on a result to view the app

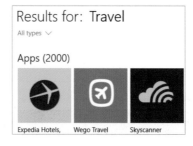

Buying Apps

When you find an app that you want to use, you can download it to your computer. To do this:

1 Access the app and click on the **Free** (or price) button

2 The app downloads from the Windows Store and a "Downloading..." message is displayed

3 The app is added to the Start menu and has a **New** tag next to it. This disappears once the app has been opened

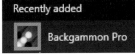

4 Click on the app to open and use it (initially it will be available under the **Recently added** section of the Start menu, as well as its own alpha listing)

Don't forget

If there is a fee for an app, this will be displayed instead of the **Free** button.

Don't forget

Once apps have been downloaded they can be reorganized and moved into different groups on the Start menu, or dragged away from their default group to start a new one (see pages 28-29).

Viewing Your Apps

As you download more and more apps from the Windows Store you may lose track of which ones you have obtained and when. To help with this, you can review all of the apps you have downloaded, from within the Windows Store. To do this:

1 Open the Windows Store and click on your account picture button at the top of the screen

2 Click on the **Downloads and updates** button

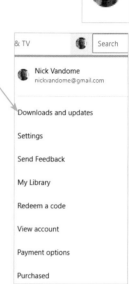

3 All of the apps that have been downloaded are displayed. Tap on the **Check for updates** button to see if there are any updates for the listed apps

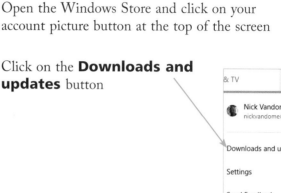

Don't forget

You can reinstall apps from the Downloads section, even if you have previously uninstalled them. If there was a fee for an app, you will not have to pay again to reinstall it.

Using Live Tiles

Before any of the Windows 10 apps have been used, they are depicted on the Start menu with tiles of solid color. However, once you open an app it activates the Live Tile feature (if it is supported by that app). This enables the tile to display real-time information from the app, even when it is not the app currently being used. This means that you can view information from your apps, directly from the Start menu. To use Live Tiles:

 Right-click on a tile to select it. If it has Live Tile functionality, click on **More** > **Turn live tile on** to activate this feature

Don't forget

The apps with Live Tile functionality include Mail, People, Calendar, Photos, Groove Music, News, Sport and Money. Some of these, such as Mail, require you to first set up an account before Live Tiles can be fully activated.

2 Live Tiles display real-time text and images from the selected apps. These are updated when there is new information available via the app

3 To turn off a Live Tile, right-click on a tile to select it and click on **More** > **Turn live tile off**

Beware

If you have too many Live Tiles activated at the same time it can become distracting and annoying, with a lot of movement on the Start menu.

Install and Uninstall

Installing apps from a CD or DVD

If the app you want to install is provided on a CD or DVD, you normally just insert the disc. The installation app starts up automatically and you can follow the instructions to select features and complete the installation. If this does not happen automatically:

Hot tip

You can access the Run function in Windows 10 by right-clicking on the **Start** button and selecting **Run** from the contextual menu.

Hot tip

Apps can also be installed from discs from File Explorer. To do this, locate the **Set-up.exe** file and double-click on it to start the installation process in the same way as in Step 2.

1   Insert the disc and click on this notification window

> DVD RW Drive (D:) CS5 Design Prem1   ✕
> Tap to choose what happens with this disc.

2   Double-click on the **Set-up.exe** file link to run it. Follow the onscreen prompts to install the app

> DVD RW Drive (D:) CS5 Des...
>
> Choose what to do with this disc.
>
> **Install or run program from your media**
>
> ◉ Run Set-up.exe
> Published by Adobe Systems Incorporated
>
> **Other choices**
>
> 📷 Import pictures and videos
> Dropbox
>
> 📂 Open folder to view files
> File Explorer
>
> 🚫 Take no action

3   Apps that are installed from a CD or DVD are added to the all apps list on the Start menu

> A
>
> A⬛ Access 2016
>
> 📄 Acer   ∨
>
> 📄 Adobe Design Premium CS5   ∧
>
> Br Adobe Bridge CS5
>
> 🔲 Adobe Device Central CS5
>
> Dw Adobe Dreamweaver CS5
>
> ⚡ Adobe ExtendScript Toolkit CS5
>
> 🔷 Adobe Extension Manager CS5
>
> ID Adobe InDesign CS5

Uninstalling apps

In some previous versions of Windows, apps were uninstalled through the Control Panel. However, in Windows 10 they can also be uninstalled directly from the Start menu. To do this:

 Right-click on an app to access its menu

 Click on the **Uninstall** button

 A window alerts you to the fact that related information will be removed if the app is uninstalled. Click on the **Uninstall** button if you want to continue

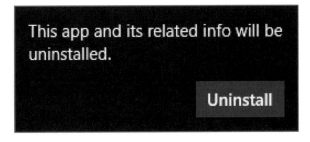

 If the app is a new Windows 10 one, or has been pinned to the Start menu (or Taskbar), its tile will be removed from its pinned location(s). For other apps, they will no longer be available from the list of apps

If apps have been installed from a CD or DVD they can also still be uninstalled from within the Control Panel. To do this, select the Programs options and click on the **Uninstall a Program** link. The installed apps will be displayed. Select one of the apps and click on the **Uninstall/Change** link.

Some elements of Windows 10, such as the Control Panel, still refer to apps as programs, but they are the same thing.

Task Manager

Task Manager lists all the apps and processes running on your computer; you can monitor performance or close an app that is no longer responding.

To open the Task Manager:

As an alternative, press **Ctrl** + **Alt** + **Delete** to display the Windows Security screen, from where you can start Task Manager.

1 Right-click on the **Start** button and select **Task Manager**, or press **Ctrl** + **Shift** + **Esc**

2 When Task Manager opens, details of the currently running apps are displayed

3 If an app is given the status of Not Responding and you cannot wait for Windows to fix things, select the app and click on the **End task** button

If an app stops responding, Windows 10 will try to find the problem and fix it automatically. Using Task Manager to end the app may be quicker, but any unsaved data will be lost.

4 Click on the **More details** button to view detailed information about the running apps. Select the **Processes** tab to show the system and the current user processes

5 The total CPU usage and the amount being used by each process are shown as (continually varying) percentages

6 Select **Performance** to see graphs of resource usage

7 The Performance panel shows graphs of the recent history of CPU and memory usage, along with other details

Alternative view

In addition to the standard view, with menus and tabs, Task Manager also has a CPU graph only view:

1 To switch to the graph only view, double-click the graph area on the Performance tab

2 To switch back to the view with menus and tabs, double-click the graph area a second time

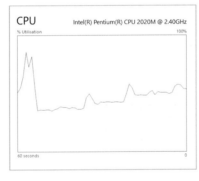

3 Select the **Wi-Fi** button in the Performance section to view the activity on your local area network. This tab also offers a graph only view

Hot tip

Resize the window so it does not take up too much space on your screen, and you can see the effects on CPU and memory as you use your system.

69

Don't forget

If you have a network adapter fitted to your computer, the Task Manager will feature a Networking tab.

Resource Monitor

The Resource Monitor provides an even more detailed view of the activities on your computer, and can be an essential aid in troubleshooting. To start the Resource Monitor:

Hot tip

Right-click any process and choose **Analyze Wait Chain...** to see which tasks are holding up an unresponsive application.

1 From Task Manager, **Performance** tab, select the **Open Resource Monitor** button

2 This displays CPU, Memory, Disk and Network details

3 For even more detail, select one of the tabs, e.g. Memory

4 Basic Controls

Even in Windows 10, much of what you do will be with menus, dialog boxes and windows, as used in numerous versions of the operating system. This chapter shows how to use these elements and how you can control and manage working with folders and files in Windows 10.

Menus

Traditionally, windows have a tabbed Menu bar near the top, displaying the menu options relevant to that particular window. Some Menu bars consist of drop-down menus and others are in the format of the Ribbon, also known as the Scenic Ribbon.

Drop-down menus

For apps such as Notepad and Calculator, the Menu bar consists of tabbed drop-down menus:

 Open the app and click, or tap, on one of the Menu bar options to view its details

Scenic Ribbon

For Windows apps, such as WordPad, (and also File Explorer and Office apps) there is a Ribbon (or Scenic Ribbon) at the top of the window with the Menu bar tabs:

 Open the app and select one of the Menu bar tabs on the Ribbon to view its details

Some options may have shortcut keys associated with them (e.g. **Alt** + **Up arrow** – Up one level), so you can use these instead of using your mouse. Other examples of shortcut keys are:

Ctrl + **A** – Select All   **Ctrl** + **C** – Copy   **Ctrl** + **V** – Paste
Ctrl + **X** – Cut   **Ctrl** + **Y** – Redo   **Ctrl** + **Z** – Undo

Dialog Boxes

Although simple actions can be made quickly from menu options, more specific settings are made from windows displayed specifically for this purpose. These are called dialog boxes.

Folder Options	✕

General | View | Search

Tabs
Some dialog boxes are divided into two or more tabs (grouped options). Only one tab can be viewed at a time.

Check boxes
Select as many as required. A tick indicates that the option is active. If you select it again it will be turned off. If an option is grayed, it is unavailable and you cannot select it.

Radio buttons
Only one out of a group of radio buttons can be selected. If you select another radio button, the previously-selected one is automatically turned off.

Click items as follows
- Single-click to open an item (point to select)
  - Underline icon titles consistent with my browser
  - Underline icon titles only when I point at them
- Double-click to open an item (single-click to select)

Command buttons
OK will save the settings selected and close the dialog box or window. **Cancel** will close, discarding any amended settings. **Apply** will save the settings selected so far but will not close, enabling you to make further changes.

OK | Cancel | Apply

Spin boxes
Spin boxes let you type or select numbers only. They usually have arrow buttons to allow you to increase or decrease the values.

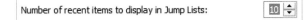
Number of recent items to display in Jump Lists: 10 ▲▼

Dialog boxes are usually fixed-size windows and therefore do not have scroll bars, minimize and maximize buttons or resize pointers.

These examples are from the Folder Options dialog box. To access it, select **Options** on the View section of the Ribbon in File Explorer and select **Change folder and search options**.

This spin box is from the Taskbar and Properties dialog box.

Structure of a Window

You can have a window containing icons for further selection, or a window that displays a screen from an app. All these windows are similar in their structure. This example is from the File Explorer.

Forward and Back

Address bar

Search box

Title bar area

Quick Access Toolbar

Command bar

Navigation pane

Minimize, Maximize/ Restore, Close

Scroll Up arrow

Slider

Scroll Down arrow

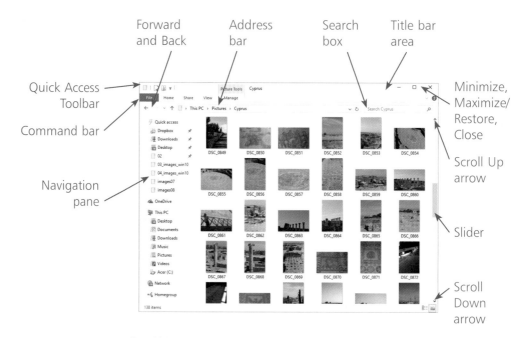

Scroll bars will only appear when there are items that cannot fit into the current size of the window. Here, only a vertical scroll bar is needed.

If you move the mouse pointer over any edge of a window, the pointer changes shape and becomes a double-headed resize arrow – drag it to change the size of a window (see page 97).

Double-click on an icon to open a window relating to it, in this case a WordPad application window. This window has a Quick access toolbar, Menu bar, Ribbon, ruler, two scroll bars, and a Control icon at the top left.

Moving a Window

As long as a window is not maximized, i.e. occupying the whole screen, you can move it. This is especially useful if you have several windows open and need to organize your Desktop.

 Move the mouse pointer over the Title bar of a window

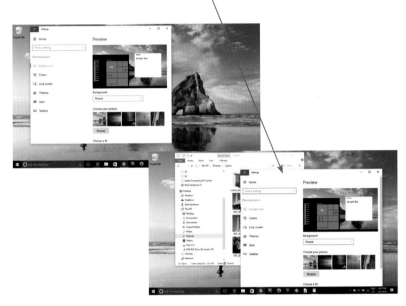

Don't forget

You will see the whole window move, with the full contents displayed, and transparency still active, while you are dragging the window.

 Drag the mouse pointer across the Desktop (left-click and hold, or tap and hold as you move)

 When the window reaches the desired location, release to relocate the window there

Control menu Move
There is a Move command for the window on the Control menu.

 Right-click the Title bar and select **Move**, and the mouse pointer changes to a four-headed arrow

 Click on the window, holding down the left mouse button and moving the pointer towards the Title bar

 The mouse pointer changes to an arrow, grabs the window and you can move and drop it as above

Hot tip

If you have two monitors attached to your system, you can extend your Desktop onto the second monitor and drag a window from one monitor onto the other.

Hot tip

If the Title bar has a Control icon, left-click this to show the menu.

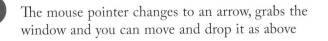

	Restore	
	Move	
	Size	
_	Minimise	
□	Maximise	
x	Close	Alt+F4

Restoring a Window

Within the Desktop environment there are a number of actions that can be performed on the windows within it. A window can be maximized to fill the whole screen, minimized to a button on the Taskbar or restored to the original size.

Original size window   Maximize button   Maximized window

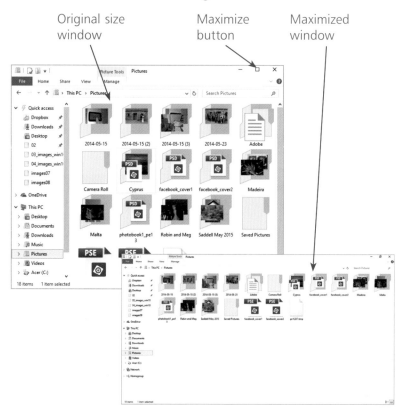

Whether a window is maximized or original size, click on the **Minimize** button (left of the top-right three buttons) to reduce the window to its Taskbar icon. This will create space on the Desktop for you to work in other windows. When you want to restore the reduced window, simply select its **Taskbar** icon.

The middle button is the Maximize button. Or, if the window is already maximized, the button changes to the Restore button.

Click **Close**, the third button, when you want to close an app or to close a window.

Resizing a Window

If a window is not maximized or minimized, it can be resized.

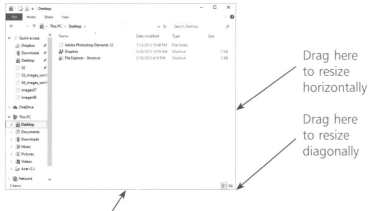

Drag here to resize horizontally

Drag here to resize diagonally

Drag here to resize vertically

Resize and move all of the windows on your Desktop to organize the layout to the way you prefer to work, or see pages 98-99 for other ways of arranging windows.

1 Place the mouse arrow anywhere on the edge of a window or on any of the corners. The pointer will change to a double-headed resize arrow

2 Click, or tap, and drag the arrow outwards to increase the size of the window, or inwards to reduce the size

Control menu Size

There is a Size command on the Control menu which makes it easier to grab the edge of the window.

	Restore	
	Move	
	Size	
	Minimize	
□	Maximize	
x	Close	Alt+F4

1 Right-click the Title bar (or left-click the Control icon) and select **Size**

2 The mouse pointer changes to a four headed arrow

3 Click the window, holding down the left mouse button, and move the pointer towards an edge or a corner of the window

4 The mouse pointer changes to a double-headed arrow and grabs the edge or corner, so you can stretch the window to the desired size, then release

Arranging Windows

If you have several windows open on your Desktop and you want to automatically rearrange them neatly, rather than resize and move each one individually, use the Cascade or Tile options.

Beware

Only open windows are arranged, not minimized windows. Also, fixed-size windows will get a proportional share of the screen, but they will not be resized.

 1 Right-click a clear area on the Taskbar to display a context menu and select one of the arrangement options

2 **Cascade windows** overlaps all open windows, revealing the Title bar areas and resizing the windows equally

Don't forget

When you right-click the Taskbar, all windows are deselected, so you must click or tap a window to select it and make it currently active.

3 **Show windows stacked** resizes windows equally and displays them across the screen in rows

4 **Show windows side by side** resizes windows equally and displays them across the screen in columns

Hot tip

When you have used a function to arrange windows, a matching Undo function is added to the Taskbar context menu.

When you have a number of windows open on the Desktop, you might wish to see what is hidden underneath. For this, Windows 10 offers the Peek function.

1   Right-click on the **Show desktop** area and select **Peek at desktop**. This will reveal outlines of the open apps whenever the cursor is moved over the Show desktop area

2   Select the **Show desktop** option in Step 1 to show just the desktop when the cursor is moved over the Show desktop area

The **Show desktop** area is on the far right of the Taskbar, next to the Notification center button.

Snap Assist

Snap Assist provides a set of methods for resizing and moving windows around the Desktop.

Maximize fully

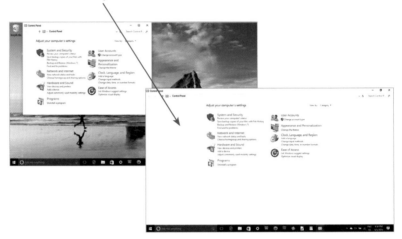

Hot tip

If the window you want to maximize is not the current one, click on it first, before carrying out the Maximize operation.

Click, or tap, and hold the Title bar and drag the window up the screen. As the mouse pointer reaches the top edge of the screen, the window maximizes. The shortcut is **WinKey** + **Up Arrow**.

Maximize vertically

Don't forget

Alternatively, you can drag the bottom border of the window towards the bottom edge of the screen.

Click, or tap, and hold the top border of the window (until it turns into a double-headed arrow) and drag it towards the top edge of the screen. When the mouse pointer reaches the edge of the screen, the window will maximize in the vertical direction only. The shortcut is **WinKey** + **Shift** + **Up Arrow**.

Snap to the left

When you click the Title bar on an app such as WordPad, be sure to avoid the tools on the Quick access toolbar.

To position the window to fill the left-hand side of the screen, click, or tap, the Title bar and drag it to the left. As the mouse pointer reaches the left edge, the window resizes to fill half of the screen. The shortcut is **WinKey** + **Left Arrow**.

Snap to the right

To position the window to fill the right-hand side of the screen, click, or tap, the Title bar and drag it to the right. As the mouse pointer reaches the right edge, the window resizes to fill half of the screen. The shortcut key is **WinKey** + **Right Arrow**.

Compare two windows

Snap one of the windows to the left and the other window to the right.

Restore

Drag the Title bar of a maximized or snapped window away from the edge of the screen and the window will return to its previous size (though not the same position). The shortcut is **WinKey** + **Down Arrow**.

Hot tip

Alternatively, to make the two windows the only open (not minimized) windows, right-click the Taskbar, and then choose the option to **Show windows side by side**.

Hot tip

Double-clicking or tapping the Title bar will also reverse the maximize or snap. This restores size and position.

Using Multiple Windows

Windows 10 provides even greater flexibility when it comes to working with windows: it is now possible to display up to four active windows at a time, rather than just two side-by-side: To do this:

 Open an app and drag its window to the left-hand side of the screen, until it snaps left and takes up the left half of the screen

Don't forget

Apps can be arranged in multiple windows in any order, e.g. one can be placed in the right-hand corner and then one on the left-hand side.

 Open a second app and drag its window to the right-hand side of the screen, until it snaps right and takes up the right half of the screen

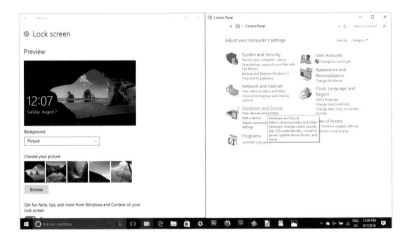

3 Open a third app and drag its window into the top left-hand corner of the screen. The left-hand side of the screen will display the two apps

4 Open a fourth app and drag its window into the top right-hand corner of the screen. The right-hand side of the screen will display the two apps

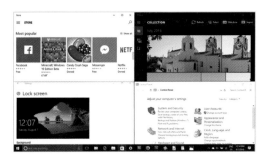

5 If other apps are open when an app is snapped into position, the Task View will display these apps in the space on the Desktop. Click on an app to expand it to fill the available space

Apps can be 'unsnapped' from their positions, by clicking and holding on the Title bar and dragging them into a new position.

Switching Windows

If you have several windows open on your Desktop, only one will be active. This will be the foremost window and it has its Title bar, Menu bar and outside window frame highlighted. If you have more than one window displayed on the Desktop, select anywhere inside a window that is not active to activate it and switch to it.

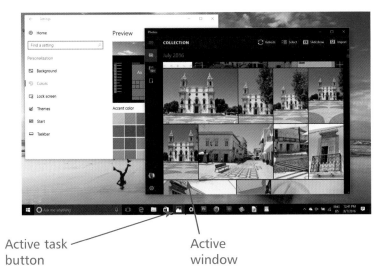

Active task ——— button

Active window

Another method of switching windows is to use the Taskbar at the bottom. Every window that is open has an icon button created automatically on the Taskbar. Therefore, it does not matter if the window you want to switch to is overlaid with others and you cannot see it. Just select the button for it in the Taskbar and the window will be moved to the front and made active.

Move the mouse pointer over a task button, and a Live Preview is displayed (one for each window if there are multiple tasks).

Don't forget

You can click on the preview to select that task and bring its window to the front of the Desktop.

Arranging Icons

You can rearrange the order of the items in your folders or on your Desktop in many different ways.

 Right-click in a clear area (of the Desktop or folder window) to display a shortcut context menu

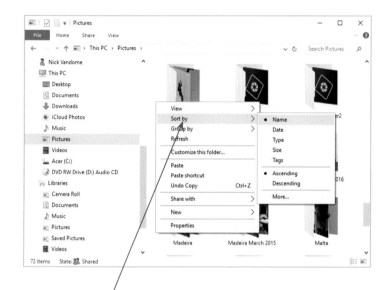

Select the **View** button to cycle through a range of views. Click, or tap, the **Down arrow** to see the full set of options.

2 Move the pointer over **Sort by** to reveal the submenu of sorting options and click or tap the **Name** option, for example, to sort all the file icons in ascending name order

3 Select **Name** a second time and the files will be sorted in descending name order

Group by

You can select **Group by** for folder windows (but not for the Desktop). This groups your files and folders alphabetically by name, size, type, etc.

Closing a Window

When you have finished with a window you will need to close it. There are several ways of doing this – use the method that is easiest and the most appropriate at the time.

Open window
If the top right corner of the window is visible on the Desktop:

 Select the **Close** button on the Title bar

Minimized window
For a window that is minimized or one that is hidden behind other windows:

 Move the mouse pointer over the associated Taskbar icon button

 Select the **Close** button on the Live Preview for the task

Control menu
If only part of the window is visible on the Desktop:

 Select the **Control** icon (top left corner) or right-click the Title bar

Select **Close** on the Control menu

Keyboard
To close any type of window use this key combination:

 Select the window to make it the current, active window, then press **Alt** + **F4** to close the window

Don't forget

Save your work before closing any app window in which you have been working. However, Windows will prompt you if you forget.

5 Customizing Windows

The Desktop environment is still an important one in Windows 10, and this chapter looks at how to work with it and personalize it to your own requirements and preferences.

Using Themes

Although more of the personalization options in Windows 10 are now applied through the Settings app, there are still some that can be set within the Control Panel. This includes the overall theme for the appearance of Windows 10.

 Open the Control Panel and click on **Change the theme**, underneath the **Appearance and Personalization** button

 Themes apply a co-ordinated color scheme for all elements on your computer

 Scroll up in the Themes window to see more options and click on a theme to apply it

Click on this link on the Themes page to obtain more from the Microsoft website

Get more themes online

Changing Sound

1 Select **Change sound effects** from **Appearance and Personalization** > **Personalization**, to see the name of the sound theme which gets applied to events in Windows

Personalization
Change the theme | Change sound effects
Change screen saver

Don't forget

Click the down-arrow on the Sound Scheme drop-down bar to try out a different scheme.

2 Select a Program Event and click the **Test** button to hear the associated sound

Hot tip

If you do not want to have sounds associated with Windows events, select **No Sounds** from the options in the drop-down list in Step 1.

3 Browse to locate a new sound file (file type .wav), then select **Test** to preview the effect

4 Make any other changes, then select **Save As**, and provide a name for your modified sound scheme

Screen Saver

With the screen saver enabled, when your mouse or keyboard has been idle for a specified period of time, Windows 10 will display a moving image or pattern. To specify the image used:

1 From **Personalization**, select the **Change screen saver** link

2 Select the **Screen saver** drop-down and choose a screen saver, e.g. Bubbles

3 Select the **Preview** button to check out the action

4 Set the time delay after which the screen saver will be invoked, and choose to display the logon screen when the system resumes

5 Click **OK** to put the screen saver into effect

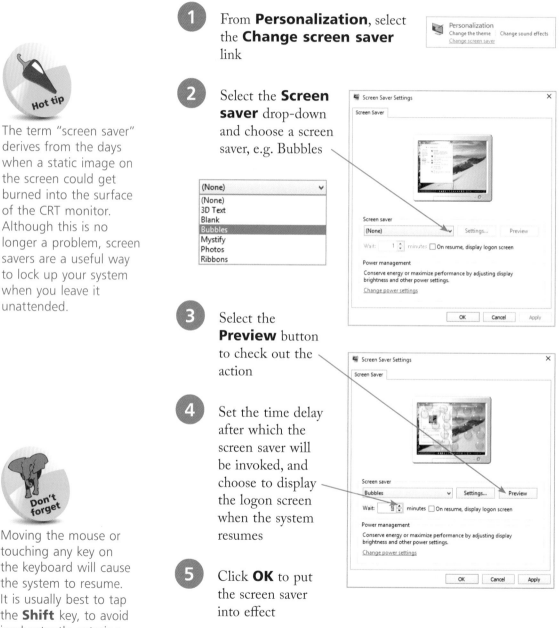

Hot tip

The term "screen saver" derives from the days when a static image on the screen could get burned into the surface of the CRT monitor. Although this is no longer a problem, screen savers are a useful way to lock up your system when you leave it unattended.

Don't forget

Moving the mouse or touching any key on the keyboard will cause the system to resume. It is usually best to tap the **Shift** key, to avoid inadvertently entering data or commands.

Desktop Icons

To control the display of icons on the Desktop:

 Right-click on the Desktop, click **View** and select **Show desktop icons**. A check mark is added

 To resize the icons, display the View menu as above and click **Large icons**, **Medium icons** or **Small icons**

To remove the check mark and hide all the icons, display the View menu and select **Show desktop icons** again

To choose which of the system icons appear, enter **Desktop icons** into the Control Panel Search box and click on the **Show or hide common icons on the desktop** link

You can use the scroll wheel on your mouse to resize desktop icons. On the Desktop, hold down **Ctrl** as you roll the wheel up or down.

Select or clear the boxes to show or hide icons as required, then click Apply and OK to confirm the changes

111

Screen Resolution

If you have a high resolution screen, you may find that the text, as well as the icons, are too small. You can increase the effective size by reducing the screen resolution.

Don't forget

If you want to use the Snap function as shown in Chapter 4 you need to have a minimum screen resolution of 1366 x 768.

Beware

If you have an LCD monitor or a laptop computer, you are recommended to stay with the native resolution, normally the highest.

1 Open the **Settings** app, select **System** and then click on the **Display** button

2 Drag this slider to change the overall size of items on your screen

3 Click the drop-down arrow next to **Orientation** to switch the view to **Portrait**, e.g. for tablet PCs

4 Click on the **Advanced display settings** link

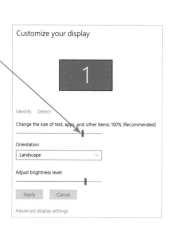

5 Click here to change the screen resolution. Select a new resolution value from the list

Resolution
1366 × 768 (Recommended)
1360 × 768
1280 × 768
1280 × 720
1280 × 600
1024 × 768
800 × 600

6 Click on the **Apply** button to change the screen resolution

Display Settings

1 Access the Control Panel and select **Appearance and Personalization** and then select **Display**

 Display
Make text and other items larger or smaller

2 Click on the **use these display settings** link to open the Settings app, where you can alter the size of the text and apps within Windows 10

🖥 Display — □ ×

← ⌄ ↑ 🖥 « Appearance and Personalization › Display ⌄ 🔍 Search Control P... 🔎

❓

Control Panel Home

Change display settings
Adjust brightness
🎨 Calibrate color
Project to a second screen
Adjust ClearType text

Change size of items

To change the size of text, apps, and other items, <u>use these display settings</u>. If you want to temporarily enlarge a portion of your screen, use <u>Magnifier</u>. If neither of these makes the changes you want, you can <u>set a custom scaling level</u> (not recommended). Setting custom levels can lead to unexpected behavior on some displays.

Change only the text size

Instead of changing the size of everything on the desktop, change only the text size for a specific item.

| Title bars | ⌄ | 10 | ⌄ | ☐ Bold |

[Apply]

See also

Personalization
Devices and Printers

113

3 Click here to change specific items, such as Title bars and Menus and click in the size box to select a specific size

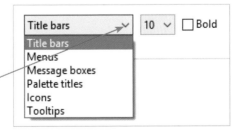

| Title bars | ⌄ | 10 ⌄ | ☐ Bold |

Title bars
Menus
Message boxes
Palette titles
Icons
Tooltips

4 Click on the **Apply** button to use the selections in Step 3

[Apply]

Hot tip

You can also select the Bold checkbox to make your display settings bold.

Ease of Access Center

1 Open **Appearance and Personalization** and select **Ease of Access Center**

2 Click on this bar to get recommendations on the settings that will be most appropriate for you

Windows will read and scan the list of common tools. Press the **Spacebar** to select the currently-highlighted tool.

3 Otherwise, scroll down to explore all of the settings. Those you select are applied automatically each time you log on

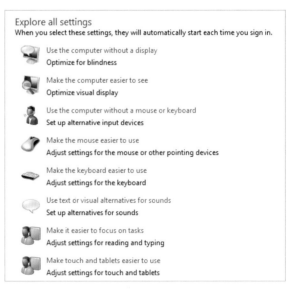

The Ease of Access Center allows you to turn on and set up apps and settings that make it easier to see your computer and use your mouse and keyboard.

...cont'd

For example, to use the Magnifier:

1 Open the Ease of Access Center and select **Start Magnifier** (or press the Spacebar while Start Magnifier is highlighted)

2 Select the **Views** drop-down button on the Magnifier toolbar to choose **Full screen**, **Lens** or **Docked** operation

The magnifier will enlarge a rectangular segment of your screen

3 Select the **Options** button on the toolbar to specify the size of the Lens area, or to specify the tracking options for the other modes of operation

4 Select **Control whether Magnifier starts when I sign in**, to turn on Magnifier at start up

Hot tip

Move the mouse pointer over the Magnifying Glass and select it to display the Magnifier toolbar.

Don't forget

To stop using Magnifier during the session, right-click the Taskbar icon and select **Close Window**.

115

Date and Time Functions

To change the format Windows uses to display dates and times:

1 Access the Control Panel, and select **Clock, Language, and Region**, and then the **Date and Time** option

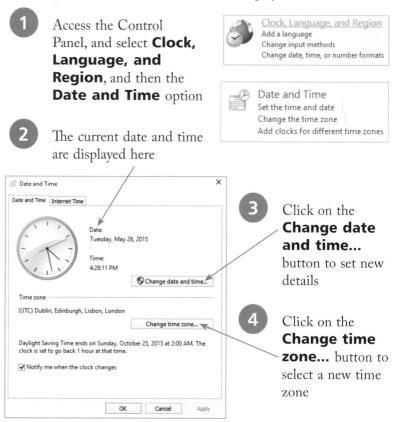

2 The current date and time are displayed here

3 Click on the **Change date and time...** button to set new details

4 Click on the **Change time zone...** button to select a new time zone

5 Click on the **Region** option (from the **Clock, Language, and Region** link in Step 1) and click on the **Formats** tab. This can be used to determine the way the time and dates are displayed

6 File Explorer

The File Explorer is at the heart of working with the files on your computer, and you can use it to browse all of the information on your computer and on the local network. This chapter shows how you can use the Scenic Ribbon function, modify the views in File Explorer, use the Quick access folder, sort the contents and customize the style and appearance.

Opening File Explorer

Although File Explorer (formerly called Windows Explorer) is not necessarily one of the first apps that you will use with Windows 10, it still plays an important role in organizing your folders and files. To access File Explorer:

This PC displays files from different locations as a single collection, without actually moving any files.

 From the Desktop, click on this icon on the Taskbar, or

 Press **WinKey** + **E**, and File Explorer opens at the **Quick access** folder

You can click on the **Start** button and access File Explorer from here too.

When File Explorer is opened, click on the **This PC** option to view the top level items on your computer, including the main folders, your hard drive and any removable devices that are connected

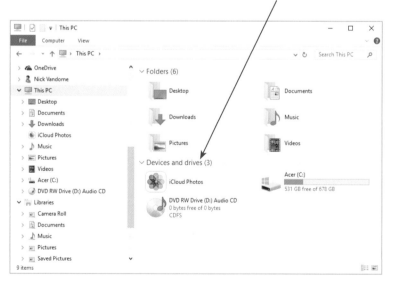

The Taskbar

The Taskbar is visible at the bottom of the screen when working in the Desktop environment. To illustrate the range of functions that it supports:

 1 Open items are displayed on the Taskbar at the bottom of  the window (denoted by a blue line underneath the item's icon)

 2 Move the mouse pointer over an open item on the Taskbar to view open files within the items and also recently viewed pages within it

 3 Move the mouse pointer over the File Explorer icon to see previews of the open folder windows that File Explorer is managing (if File Explorer is open)

Hot tip

File Explorer (also known as Explorer) is the program Explorer.exe. It handles the file system and user interfaces, and is sometimes referred to as the Windows Shell.

Hot tip

When you right-click the Desktop, you will find customization functions, Display settings and Personalization on the context menu displayed.

Libraries

File Explorer can use the Library for accessing the files and folders on your computer and network. Each Library displays files from several locations. Initially there are five Libraries defined:

- **Camera Roll**, which is the default folder for photos captured on your computer (if it has a camera attached).

- **Documents**, which is the default folder for files such as those created with word processing or presentation apps.

- **Music**, which is the default folder for music bought from the online Windows Store, or added yourself.

- **Pictures**, which is the default folder for your photos.

- **Videos**, which is the default folder for your videos.

Beware

In Windows 10 the Libraries are not visible by default. To show them, click on the **Navigation pane** button and click on the **Show libraries** button so that a tick appears.

To view the Pictures library, for example:

 Select **Libraries > Pictures** in the Navigation pane

To add another folder to the Pictures library:

1 Right-click in the Pictures library window and select **New > Folder**

2 Click on the folder name and overwrite it with a new title

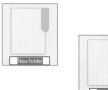

120

Hot tip

You can also right-click the folder name in the Navigation pane folder list, to display the **New > Folder** menu.

Scenic Ribbon

The navigation and functionality in the Libraries is provided by the Scenic Ribbon at the top of the window. This has options for the Library itself and also the type of content that is being viewed.

 1 Click on the tabs at the top of the Library window to view associated tools

 2 Click on the Library Tools tab to view the menus for the whole Library (see below)

3 Click on the content tab (Picture Tools in this example) to view menus for the selected content

Library File menu

This contains options for opening a new window, closing the current window or moving to a frequently-visited location in the Library.

Library Home menu

This contains options for copying and pasting, moving, deleting and renaming selected items. You can also create new folders, view folder properties and select all items in a folder.

The Scenic Ribbon is also referred to as just the Ribbon.

The **File** button in the Ribbon remains highlighted in blue, regardless of which other menu is accessed.

...cont'd

Library Share menu

This contains options for sharing selected items, by sending them to the HomeGroup or another user on the computer, burning them to a CD or DVD, creating a compressed Zip file or sending the items to a printer.

Library View menu

This contains options for how you view the items in the current active folder (see page 132).

Hot tip

Click on the **Options** button on the View menu to set additional options for the operation of a folder and how items are displayed within it.

Library Manage menu

This contains options for managing specific libraries. Click on the **Manage library** button to add additional folders to the one currently being viewed.

Library menu options

If there is a down-pointing arrow next to an item on a Library menu click it to see additional options, such as the **Optimize library for** button, which optimizes the folder for specific types of content.

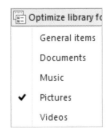

This PC Folder

One of the best ways to look at the contents of your computer involves using the This PC folder. To open this:

1 Open File Explorer and select **This PC** in the Navigation pane

Navigation pane   Location   Search box

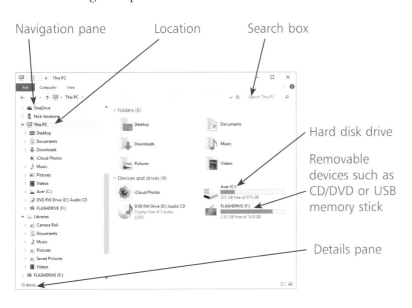

Hard disk drive

Removable devices such as CD/DVD or USB memory stick

Details pane

The Navigation pane provides the facilities you require to move between folders and drives.

2 Select items and double-click to view their contents

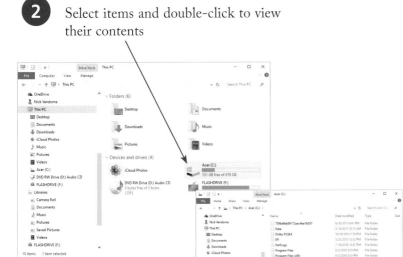

Quick Access

When working with files and folders there will probably be items which you access on a regular basis. The Quick access section of the File Explorer can be used to view the items that you have most recently accessed, and also to pin your most frequently used and favorite items. To use the Quick access section:

1 Click on the **Quick access** button in the File Explorer Navigation pane so that the right-pointing arrow becomes downwards-pointing

2 In the main window, your frequently used folders and most recently used files are displayed

Don't forget

The items displayed under Quick access are not physically located here; the links are just shortcuts to the actual location within your file structure.

Hot tip

To view the actual location of a file, right-click on it within Quick access and click on **Open file location** from the menu.

124

3 The folders are also listed underneath the **Quick access** button in the Navigation pane

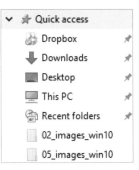

Adding items to Quick access

The folders that you access and use most frequently can be pinned to the Quick access section. This does not physically move them; it just creates a shortcut within Quick access. To do this:

1 Right-click on the folder you want to pin and click on **Pin to Quick access**

Windows 10

> **Open**
> Open in new window
> Pin to Quick access

2 The folder is pinned to the Quick access section, which is denoted by the pin symbol; or

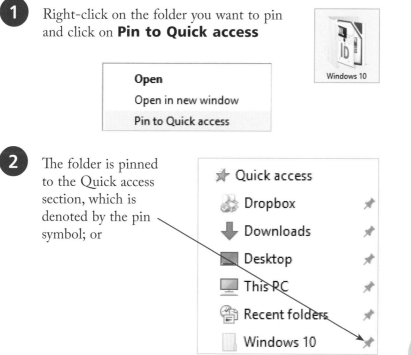

★ Quick access
Dropbox
Downloads
Desktop
This PC
Recent folders
Windows 10

3 Drag the folder over the Quick access button until the **Pin to Quick access** option appears, and release

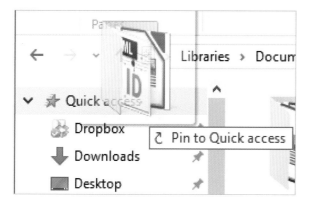

Libraries › Docum

✓ ★ Quick access
Dropbox
Downloads
Desktop

↻ Pin to Quick access

Don't forget

To unpin an item from Quick access, right-click on it and click on **Unpin from Quick access**.

125

Exploring Drives

Explore the contents of any drive from the This PC folder:

 Select one
of the drive
icons – for
example, the
Flashdrive
removable
storage device

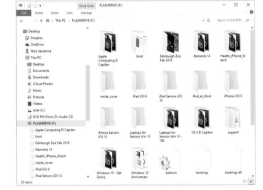

 Double-
click the
Flashdrive
device icon
(or select it
and press
Enter) to
display the
files and
folders that it
contains

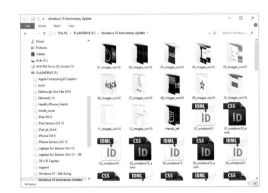

 Double-
click a folder
entry (e.g.
Windows 10
Anniversary
Update) and
select one of
the files that
it contains

Double-click the file icon and press **Enter** to open the
file using the associated application

Don't forget

Press the **Back arrow**
to go to the previous
library or location, or
click the **Down arrow**
to select from the list of
viewed locations. Click
the **Up arrow** to move
up one level.

126

...cont'd

You can see all the folder entries in This PC in a structured list:

 Double-click the **This PC** entry in the Navigation pane

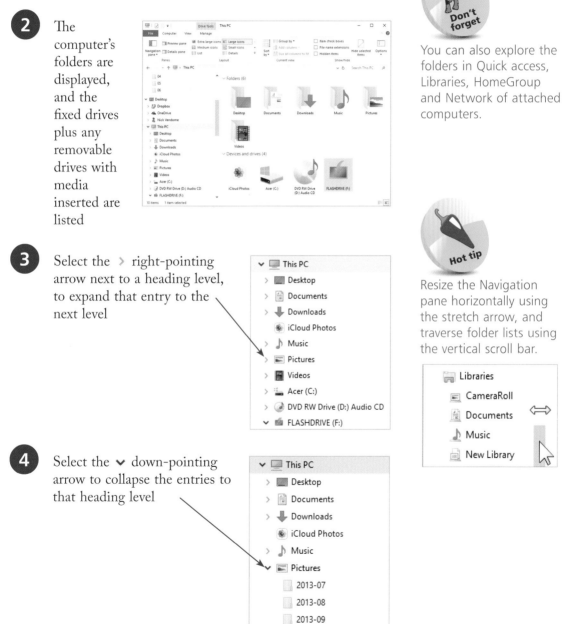

2 The computer's folders are displayed, and the fixed drives plus any removable drives with media inserted are listed

3 Select the › right-pointing arrow next to a heading level, to expand that entry to the next level

4 Select the ✓ down-pointing arrow to collapse the entries to that heading level

You can also explore the folders in Quick access, Libraries, HomeGroup and Network of attached computers.

Don't forget

Hot tip

Resize the Navigation pane horizontally using the stretch arrow, and traverse folder lists using the vertical scroll bar.

127

Address Bar

The Address bar at the top of File Explorer displays the current location as a set of names separated by arrows, and offers another way to navigate between libraries and locations.

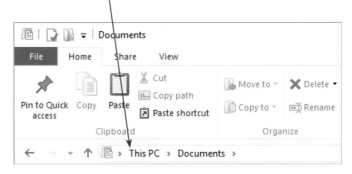

1 To go to a location that is named in the address, click on that name in the Address bar, e.g. Documents

2 To select a subfolder of a library or location named in the Address bar, click on the arrow to the right

3 Click one of the entries to open it in place of the current location

When you are viewing a drive rather than a library, the Address bar shows the drive and its folders, and allows you to navigate amongst these.

You can specify a new location using the Address bar:

 Click on the Address bar in the blank space to the right of the set of names, and the full path is displayed

← → ⌄ ↑ 📄 › This PC › Documents ›

 Type the complete folder path, e.g. C:\Users\Public (or click in the path and amend the values), then press Enter

Hot tip

The path is highlighted, so typing a new path will completely replace the original values.

← → ⌄ ↑ 🗆 C:\Users\Public|

3 The specified location will be displayed

← ⌄ ↑ 🗆 › This PC › Acer (C:) › Users › Public ›

	Name	Date modified
This PC	Public Documents	5/21/2015 12:48 AM
Desktop	Public Downloads	3/14/2015 8:58 AM
Documents	Public Music	3/14/2015 8:58 AM
Downloads	Public Pictures	3/14/2015 8:58 AM
Music	Public Videos	3/14/2015 8:58 AM
Pictures	NTUSER.DAT	1/14/2015 1:29 PM
Videos		
Acer (C:)		

If you want a common location such as Desktop, just type the name alone and press **Enter**, and the location will be displayed:

← → ⌄ ↑ 🗆 desktop|
　　　　　　　　Desktop
Music　　　　Search for "desktop"
Pictures

Hot tip

You can switch to exploring the internet, by typing a web page address. Windows Edge will be launched in a separate window.

Navigation Panes

The normal view for File Explorer includes the Navigation pane. There is also a Preview pane and a Details pane available.

You can choose different panes to display:

 Open File Explorer and click on the **View** tab. This will open the Ribbon

 The Pane options are located at the left-hand side of the Ribbon

3 Click on the **Navigation pane** button to view this format. This appears down the left-hand side

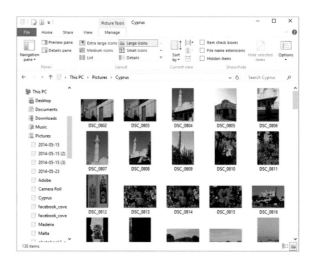

4 Click on the arrow on the **Navigation pane** button and click here to show or hide the Navigation pane. There are also options here for showing or hiding the libraries

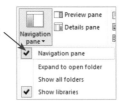

5 Click on the **Preview pane** button to view a preview of the folder or file selected in the main window

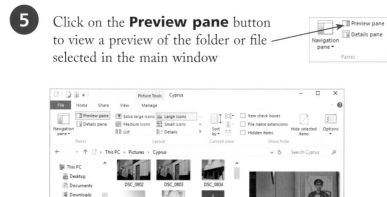

The Preview pane is particularly useful if you are working in the Pictures library.

Don't forget

6 Click on the **Details pane** button to view additional information about the folder or file selected in the main window

Changing Views

You can change the size and appearance of the file and folder icons in your folders, using the View tab on the Ribbon.

 Open the folder you would like to change and click on the **View** tab on the Ribbon. Select one of the options for viewing content in the folder

View	Manage
Extra large icons	Large icons
Medium icons	Small icons
List	Details
Layout	

The way items are displayed within folders can also be set within Folder Options (see page 136).

132

 Click on different items to change the appearance of icons, such as from the Layout section

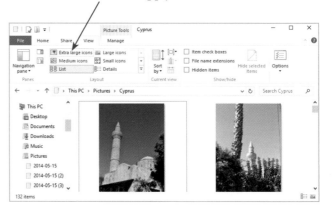

Hover the cursor over each View setting to preview. Click the mouse button to apply that view

Sorting

Windows 10 allows you to sort your files in the drive or folder by various attributes or descriptors.

 Open the folder, click on **View > Details** and select the attribute header that you want to sort by, e.g. Date

 The entries are sorted into ascending order by the selected attribute. The header is shaded and a sort symbol ⌃ added

	Name	Date
This PC		
Desktop		
Documents	DSC_0808	11/10/2014 1:41 AM
Downloads	DSC_0809	11/10/2014 1:43 AM
Music	DSC_0810	11/10/2014 1:43 AM
Pictures	DSC_0811	11/10/2014 1:43 AM
	DSC_0812	11/10/2014 1:45 AM
	DSC_0813	11/10/2014 3:18 AM

This PC › Pictures › Cyprus

 Select the header again. The order is reversed and the header now shows an inverted sort symbol ⌄

	Name	Date
This PC		
Desktop	hobbit_house1	11/11/2014 12:29 AM
Documents	DSC_0934	12/2/2014 2:01 AM
Downloads	DSC_0933	12/2/2014 2:00 AM
Music	DSC_0932	11/13/2014 2:22 AM
Pictures	DSC_0931_1	11/13/2014 2:22 AM
	DSC_0931	11/13/2014 2:22 AM

This PC › Pictures › Cyprus

Hot tip

Note that any subfolders within your folder will be sorted to the end of the list, when you reverse the sequence. Libraries are an exception, and keep folders at the top (in the appropriate sort order).

133

4 The contents will remain sorted in the selected sequence, even if you switch to a different folder view

This PC › Pictures › Cyprus

This PC	hobbit_house1 DSC_0927 DSC_0918	
Desktop	DSC_0934 DSC_0926 DSC_0917	
Documents	DSC_0933 DSC_0925 DSC_0916	
Downloads	DSC_0932 DSC_0924 DSC_0915	
	DSC_0931_1 DSC_0923 DSC_0914	

Filtering

 1 In the Details view (see page 132), select any header and click the **Down arrow** to the right-hand side

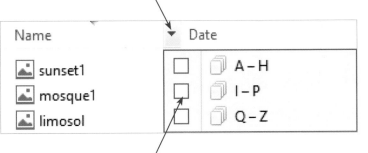

 2 Select a box next to one or more ranges, and the items displayed are immediately restricted to that selection

3 You can select a second header, Size for example, to apply additional filtering to the items displayed

Size		Tags
3,648 K	☐	Medium (100 KB - 1 MB)
728 K	☐	Large (1 - 16 MB)
6,342 K	☐	Huge (16 - 128 MB)

 4 The tick ✔ symbol on headers indicates that filtering is in effect, and the Address bar shows the attributes

> This PC ▸ Pictures ▸ Cyprus ▸ Large (1 - 16 MB)

^ Name   Date

5 Filtering remains in effect even if you change folder views, within the selected folder

Hot tip

This shows ranges of values appropriate to the particular attribute and based on the actual contents of the folder. These ranges are used for filtering and for grouping the items in the folder.

Hot tip

Filtering can only be applied in the Details folder view.

Beware

If you navigate away from the folder or close File Explorer, the next time you visit the folder, the filtering will have been removed.

134

Grouping

You can group the contents of a folder using the header ranges.
You do not need to select the Details view.

 Right-click an empty part of the folder area, select
Group by, then select an attribute, e.g. **Type**

The right-click context
menu also offers the
Sort by option, so you
can specify or change
the sort sequence
without switching to
Details view.

 The contents will
be grouped, using
the ranges for the
attribute selected

Any sorting that was
already in place will
remain in effect.
However, you can switch
between **Ascending**
and **Descending**.

Grouping is retained when you switch views (and when
you revisit the folder after closing File Explorer)

Select **Group by** >
(None) to remove
grouping. Select
More... to add other
attributes. The new
attributes will also
appear in Details view.

You can regroup the folder contents by selecting another
attribute. This will replace your original choice

Folder Options

You can change the appearance and the behavior of your folders by adjusting the folder settings.

 1 From the View tab on the Ribbon, click on the **Options** button and select the **Change folder and search options** link

2 Choose **Open each folder in its own window**, to keep multiple folders open at the same time

Folder Options ✕

General | View | Search

Open File Explorer to: Quick access ▾

Browse folders

○ Open each folder in the same window
● Open each folder in its own window

Click items as follows

○ Single-click to open an item (point to select)
  ○ Underline icon titles consistent with my browser
  ● Underline icon titles only when I point at them
● Double-click to open an item (single-click to select)

Privacy

☑ Show recently used files in Quick access
☑ Show frequently used folders in Quick access

Clear File Explorer history   Clear

Restore Defaults

OK | Cancel | Apply

3 If you want items to open as they do on a web page, select **Single-click to open an item (point to select)**

4 Select the **View** tab to select options for how items appear in the File Explorer libraries

5 Select **Apply** to try out the selected changes without closing the Folder Options, then OK to confirm

Apply

6 Alternatively, select **Restore Defaults** then **Apply**, to reset all options to their default values

Restore Defaults

7 Managing Files and Folders

Folders can contain other folders as well as files, and Windows 10 treats them in very much the same way. Hence, operations such as moving, copying, deleting and searching apply to files and to folders in a similar way. This chapter shows how to perform these tasks and actions while working with folders and files within File Explorer.

Select Files and Folders

Single file or folder

To process several files or folders, it is more efficient to select and process them as a group, rather than one by one.

 Click the item to highlight it, then move, copy or delete it as required

Sequential files

Use the sorting, filtering and grouping options (see pages 133-135) to rearrange the files to make the selection easier.

 Click to select the first item, press and hold **Shift**, then click the last item, to highlight the range

Adjacent block

You must start the selection box from an empty space in the folder. If you accidently click a file or folder, you will drag that item, rather than create a box.

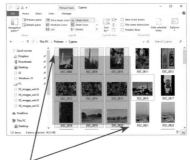

 Drag out a box to cover the files you want selected. All of the files in the rectangular area will be highlighted

Non-adjacent files

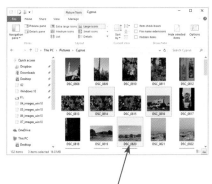

1 To select several, non-adjacent files, click one item, press and hold **Ctrl**, then click the subsequent items. As you select files, they are highlighted

Partial sequence

You can combine these techniques to select part of a range.

1 Select a group of sequential files or an adjacent block of files (as described on the previous page)

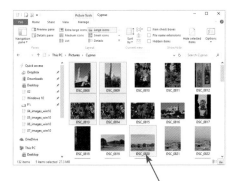

Hot tip

To deselect one file, click it while the **Ctrl** key is being held down. To deselect all of the files, click once anywhere in the folder outside of the selection area.

2 Hold down **Ctrl** and click to deselect any files in the range that you do not want, and to select extra ones

All files and folders

To select all of the files (and folders) in the current folder, select the **Home** tab on the Ribbon and click on **Select All** or press **Ctrl** + **A**.

Beware

If you select a folder, you will also be selecting any files and folders that it may contain.

Copy or Move Files or Folders

You may wish to copy or move files and folders to another folder on the same drive, or to another drive. There are several ways to achieve this:

Drag, using the right mouse button

For ease and simplicity, the prompted method using the right mouse button is recommended.

 Open File Explorer and the folder with the required files, then locate the destination in the Folders list in the Navigation pane

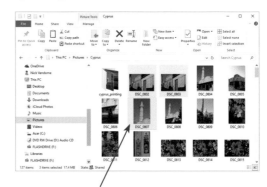

 In the folder contents, select the files and folders that you want to copy or move

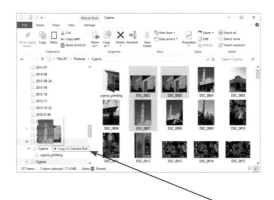

 Right-click any one of the selection, drag the files onto the destination folder or drive in the Folders list, so it is highlighted and named, then release to display the menu

 Click the **Move here** or **Copy here** option as desired, and the files will be added to the destination folder

| Copy here |
| **Move here** |
| Create shortcuts here |
| Cancel |

Drag, using the left mouse button

In this case, default actions are applied with no intervening menu.

 Select the files and folders to be moved or copied

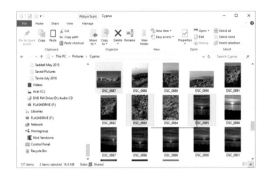

Hot tip

Open File Explorer and the source folder, then locate the destination in the Folders list in the Navigation pane, ready for moving or copying files and folders.

 Use the left mouse button to drag the selection to the destination drive or folder in the Folders list – in this example, the removable USB storage drive (Flashdrive)

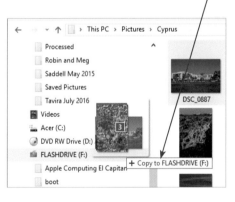

Hot tip

As you hover over a drive or folder in the Folders list in the Navigation pane, it expands to reveal the subfolders.

 Press **Shift** to Move instead of Copy to another drive. Press **Ctrl** to Copy instead of Move to a folder on the same drive as the source folder

Don't forget

You will see a ✚ symbol if the file is going to be copied, or a ➜ if the file is going to be moved.

In summary

Drives	Drag	Drag+Shift	Drag+Ctrl
Same	Move	Move	Copy
Different	Copy	Move	Copy

...cont'd

Using Cut, Copy and Paste

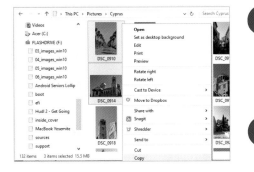

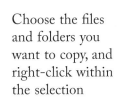

Hot tip

Cut does not remove the selection initially, it just dims it, until you Paste it (see Step 5). Press **Esc** if you decide to cancel the move, and the item will remain in place.

1 Choose the files and folders you want to copy, and right-click within the selection

2 From the context menu, click **Copy** or **Cut** to move the selection

3 Move to the destination folder (or create a new one)

4 Right-click a blank area of the destination folder

5 Select **Paste** from the menu to complete the Copy or move operation

Don't forget

When you Copy, you can **Paste shortcut** (instead of Paste) to insert a link to the original file. However, this is inactive when you Cut files.

Keyboard shortcuts

Cut, Copy and Paste options are also available as keyboard shortcuts. Select files and folders as above, but use these keys in place of the menu selections for Copy, Cut and Paste. There are also shortcuts to Undo an action or Redo an action.

Press this key	To do this
F1	Display Help
Ctrl+C	Copy the selected item
Ctrl+X	Cut the selected item
Ctrl+V	Paste the selected item
Ctrl+Z	Undo an action
Ctrl+Y	Redo an action

Burn to disc

If your computer has a CD or DVD recorder, you can copy files to a writable disc. This is usually termed "burning".

1 Insert a writable CD or DVD disc into the recorder drive (DVD/CD RW). Click on this pop-up

2 When the prompt appears, choose the option to **Burn files to disc** using File Explorer

DVD RW Drive (D:)

Choose what to do with blank DVDs.

Burn files to disc
File Explorer

Take no action

3 Make sure the CD/DVD is selected and copy and paste files into the main window, or drag files there to copy them to the disc, or

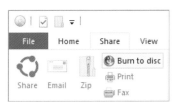

You can use any of the methods described for copying or moving one or more files and folders (see pages 140-142).

4 Select files within another File Explorer window and click on the **Burn to disc** button under the **Share** tab

File Conflicts

When you copy or move files from one folder to another, conflicts may arise. There may already be a file with the same name in the destination folder. To illustrate what may happen:

 Open a folder, e.g. **Documents > Windows 10 Anniversary Update** folder and the USB Flashdrive

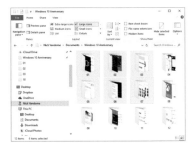

 Press **Ctrl** + **A** to select all of the files and drag them onto the Flashdrive, to initiate a copy of them

 Windows observes a conflict – some files already exist, with identical size and date information. Select one of the options

Hot tip

You can, of course, use the Copy and Paste options from the right-click menus, or use the equivalent keyboard shortcuts, and File Explorer will continue to check for possible conflicts.

If you select the **Let me decide for each file** option, details will be displayed so you can view if one is newer than another. Click on the **Continue** button to confirm the decisions made

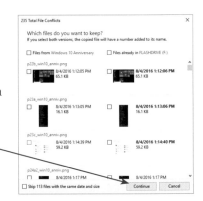

Open Files

You can open a file using an associated app without first having to explicitly start that app. There are several ways to do this:

Default program

 Double-click the file icon, or

 Right-click the file and select **Open** from the menu, or

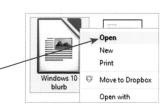

Hot tip

Default programs can also be set in **Control Panel** > **Programs** > **Default programs**.

Select the file, then click **Open** from the Home tab of the Ribbon. This will open the file in its default app

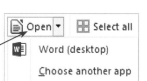

Alternative program (app)

You may have several apps that can open a particular file type. To use a different app than the default to open the file:

 Right-click the file icon and select **Open with**. Pick an app from the list or click **Choose another app** to set a new default app

	Print		
🗘	Move to Dropbox		
	Open with	>	W〕 Word (desktop)
	Share with	>	Choose another app

The same choices are presented when you select the down arrow next to the **Open** button on the Ribbon in the folder window

Delete Files and Folders

When you want to remove files or folders, you use the same delete procedures – whatever drive or device the items are stored on.

 1 Choose one or more files and folders, selected as described previously (see pages 138-139)

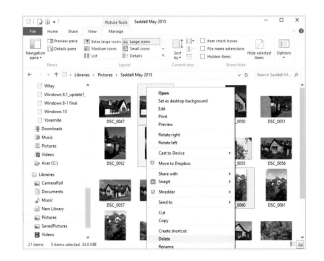

Don't forget

When you delete files and folders from your hard disk drive, they are actually moved to a temporary storage area, the Recycle Bin (see next page).

Hot tip

You can press the **Delete** key on your keyboard, after selecting the files and folders, instead of using the menus or Ribbon.

2 Right-click the selection and click **Delete**

3 Alternatively, click on the **Delete** button on the Ribbon, or click the arrow and select one of the options

Don't forget

You may need to have administrator authority to delete some files or folders from your system.

If you choose to delete and then immediately realize that you have made a mistake deleting one or more files, right-click the folder area and select **Undo Delete** or press **Ctrl** + **Z**, to reverse the last operation. For hard disk items, you are also able to retrieve deleted files from the Recycle Bin, and this could be a substantial time later (unless you have emptied or bypassed the Recycle Bin – see pages 148-149).

The Recycle Bin

The Recycle Bin is, in effect, a folder on your hard disk that holds deleted files and folders. They are not physically removed from your hard disk (unless you empty the Recycle Bin or delete specific items from within the Recycle Bin itself). They will remain there until the Recycle Bin fills up, at which time the oldest deleted files may finally be removed.

The Recycle Bin, therefore, provides a safety net for files and folders you may delete by mistake, and allows you to easily retrieve them, even at a later date.

Restoring files

 Double-click on the **Recycle Bin** icon from the Desktop or in the Navigation pane

Recycle Bin

Don't forget

To see where the Recycle Bin is located, right-click in a clear areaa of the **Navigation pane** and select **Show all folders**.

✓ Show libraries
✓ Show all folders
    Expand to current folder

 Select the **Restore all items** button, or select a file and the button changes to **Restore this item**

Hot tip

A restored folder will include all the files and subfolders that it held when it was originally deleted.

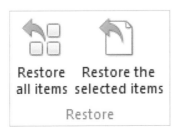

...cont'd

Permanently erase files

You may want to explicitly delete particular files, perhaps for reasons of privacy and confidentiality.

 Open the Recycle Bin

 Select the relevant files and folders, then select **Delete** from the one of the menus (or press the **Delete** key)

 Select **Yes**, to confirm that you want to permanently delete these files (completely remove them from the hard disk)

Empty the Recycle Bin

If desired, you can remove all of the contents of the Recycle Bin from the hard disk:

 With the Recycle Bin open, select the **Empty Recycle Bin** button

Empty
Recycle Bin

 Press **Yes** to confirm the permanent deletion

The Recycle Bin icon changes from full to empty, to illustrate the change.

Don't forget

You do not have to worry about the space used in the Recycle Bin. Windows keeps track and removes the oldest deleted entries when the maximum allowed space, typically 10% of the drive, has been used.

Hot tip

Right-click the Recycle Bin icon and select **Empty Recycle Bin**, to remove all of the files and folders without it being open.

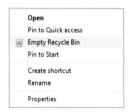

Bypass the Recycle Bin

If you want to prevent particular deleted files from being stored in the Recycle Bin:

 From their original location, select the files and folders, right-click the selection, but this time hold down the **Shift** key as you select **Delete**

| Cut |
| Copy |
| Create shortcut |
| Delete |
| Rename |

Hot tip

You could also just press the **Delete** key on the keyboard to delete items or **Shift** + the **Delete** key to delete items permanently.

 Confirm that you want to permanently delete the selected item or items. 'Permanent' means that no copy will be kept

Delete File   ✕

Are you sure you want to permanently delete this file?

DSC_0051
Item type: JPG File
Date taken: 3/10/2014 5:43 AM
Rating: Unrated
Dimensions: 4608 x 3072
Size: 7.07 MB

Yes   No

Deactivate (or resize) the Recycle Bin

You can tell Windows to always bypass the Recycle Bin:

Beware

Take extra care when selecting files and folders if you are bypassing the Recycle Bin, since you will have no recovery options.

1 Right-click the Recycle Bin icon, then select **Properties** from the menu

Open
Pin to Quick access
Empty Recycle Bin
Pin to Start
Create shortcut
Rename
Properties

2 Note the space available in the Recycle Bin location (free space on hard disk)

3 Adjust the maximum size allowed, to resize the Recycle Bin

Recycle Bin Properties   ✕

General

Recycle Bin Location   Space Available
Acer (C:)   678 GB

Settings for selected location
● Custom size:
   Maximum size (MB):   36804
○ Don't move files to the Recycle Bin. Remove files immediately when deleted.

☐ Display delete confirmation dialog

OK   Cancel   Apply

4 Click the button labeled **Don't move files to the Recycle Bin. Remove files immediately when deleted**, to always bypass the Recycle Bin

Create a Folder

You can create a new folder in a drive, folder or on the Desktop:

1 Right-click an empty part of the folder window, select **New** and then **Folder**

Don't forget

Make sure that you click in the space between icons, away from the (usually hidden) boxes surrounding the icons.

2 Overtype the default name New Folder, e.g. type *Articles*, and press **Enter**

Beware

If you click away from the icon without typing the new name, you get folders called New Folder, New Folder (2) and so on.

You can also create a new file in a standard format for use with one of the apps installed on your computer:

1 Right-click an empty part of the folder, select **New**, and choose the specific file type, e.g. Text Document file

Don't forget

Normally, the file name extension (which shows the file type) will be hidden. To reveal file extensions, open **Folder Options**, select the **View** tab and clear the box labeled **Hide extensions for known file types**.

2 Overtype the file name provided and press **Enter**

Rename a File or Folder

You can rename a file or folder at any time, by simply editing the current name:

1 Right-click the file/folder, then click **Rename**, or select the icon and click on the icon name

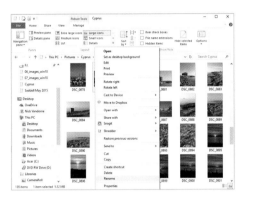

Hot tip

Use the same method to rename icons on the Desktop. You can even rename the Recycle Bin.

Recycle Bin

2 Either way, the current name will be highlighted. Type a name to delete and replace the current name, or press the arrow keys to position the typing cursor and edit the existing name:

Don't forget

You must always provide a non-blank file name, and you should avoid special characters such as quote marks, question marks and periods.

3 Press **Enter** or click elsewhere to confirm the new name

Preserving file types

When you have file extensions revealed and you create or rename a file or folder, only the name itself, not the file type, will be highlighted. This avoids accidental changes of type.

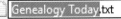
Genealogy Today.txt

Genealogy.txt

Beware

You can change the file type (extension), but you will be warned that this may make the file unusable.

151

Backtrack File Operations

If you accidentally delete, rename, copy or move the wrong file or folder, you can undo (reverse) the last operation and preceding operations, to get back to where you started. For example:

Undo mistakes as soon as possible since you would have to undo subsequent operations first. Also, only a limited amount of undo history is maintained.

The Undo command that is offered changes depending on which operation was being performed at the time.

If you go back too far, right-click the folder and select the available Redo operation, e.g. Redo Rename.

Undo commands do not work on permanently deleted files.

 Right-click the folder area and select the **Undo Rename** command that is displayed

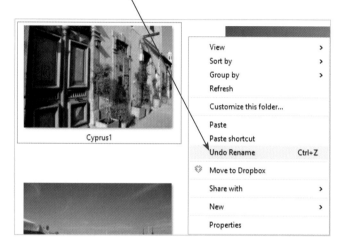

 Right-click again, and this time there is an **Undo Delete** command for you to select

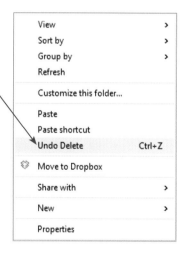

 Now you will have reversed the last two operations, putting the folder and files back as they were before the changes

152

File Properties

Every file (and every folder) has information that can be displayed in the Properties dialog box. To display this:

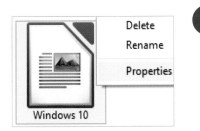

1 Right-click the file or folder icon to display the shortcut menu

2 Select the **Properties** option, to display details for the file

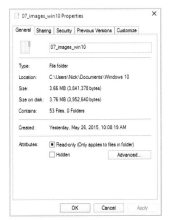

3 Right-click a folder icon and select **Properties**, to display the folder information

4 Similarly, you can display Properties for any of the Libraries

The purpose of the Properties dialog box is:
- to display details
- to change settings for the selected file or folder.

Click **Security** and the other tabs, to display more information about the file or folder, and click the **Advanced...** button for additional attributes.

In View mode on the Ribbon, select a folder and select the **Options** button. Then select the **Change folder and search options** link to view folder Properties.

Search for Files and Folders

If you are not quite sure where exactly you stored a file, or what the full name is, the File Explorer Search box may be the answer.

 Open a location, e.g. Documents, click in the Search box and start typing a word from the file, e.g. *Nick*

Open the library or folder that is most likely to hold the file you want, then click in the Search box to initiate a search, looking at file names and content, limited to that folder and its subfolders.

Some files contain the search words in the file names, while others contain the words within the textual content.

For an attached hard drive, you may be offered the option to **Click to add to index**, and thereby speed up future searches. Indexing is the process of the Search facility storing the words that can be searched over.

If that produces too many files, start typing another word that might help limit the number of matches, e.g. *Vandome*

If the location is a drive rather than a library, its contents may not be indexed, so the search may take longer

You can also use Cortana to search for files and folders (see pages 60-61).

Compressed Folders

This feature allows you to save disk space by compressing files and folders, while allowing them to be treated as normal by Windows 10.

Create a compressed folder

 Right-click an empty portion of the folder window and select **New > Compressed (zipped) Folder**

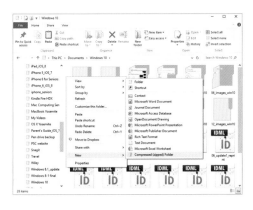

 A compressed folder is created, with the default name New Compressed (zipped) Folder.zip

 Rename it (see page 151). You can also open, move, or delete it just like any other folder

New Compressed (zipped) Folder

Add files or folders to a compressed folder

 Drag files or folders onto a compressed folder and they will automatically be compressed and stored there

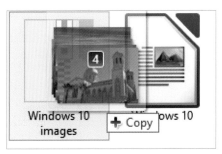

Hot tip

Compressed folders are distinguished from other folders by a zipper on the folder icon. They are compatible with other zip archive apps, such as WinZip.

Don't forget

To create a compressed folder and copy a file into it at the same time: right-click a file, select **Send To > Compressed (zipped) folder**. The new compressed folder has the same file name, but with a file extension of .zip.

...cont'd

Compressed item Properties

 Double-click the compressed folder and select any file to see the actual size versus the compressed size

Right-click the file and select **Properties** to display this information, if the Details panel has not been enabled (see page 132).

Extract files and folders

 Open the compressed folder, drag files and folders onto a normal folder and they will be decompressed. The compressed version still remains in the compressed folder, unless you hold the Shift key as you drag (i.e. Move)

Extract all

 To extract all of the files and folders from a compressed folder, right-click it and then click on **Extract all** or select it from the Extract section on the Ribbon

Extract
all

If the folder specified does not exist, it will be created automatically.

Accept or edit the target folder and click **Extract**. The files and folders are decompressed and transferred

Fonts Folder

Windows includes several hundred different fonts. These offer a wide range of distinctive and artistic effects in windows and documents, and support multiple languages and special symbols.

To view the fonts available on your system:

1 Access the Control Panel and open **Fonts** from **Appearance and Personalization**

2 The Fonts folder is displayed

3 Double-click on a group font such as Arial to see the font styles that it contains

You can also find the Fonts folder within the C:\Windows folder.

Double-click on a font to see samples of the characters at various point sizes.

Character Map

As well as letters and numbers, the fonts contain many special characters, not all of which appear on your computer keyboard. You can insert these characters into your documents using the Character Map, or by pressing particular key combinations.

 1 In the Fonts folder select **Find a character** to display the Character Map application

Find a character

Change font size

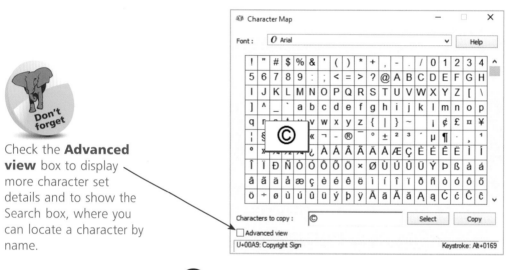

Check the **Advanced view** box to display more character set details and to show the Search box, where you can locate a character by name.

 2 Select any character to see an enlarged version. The key combination and description is shown on the Status bar

 3 Click **Select** to add the character to the copy box, and click **Copy** to transfer it to the clipboard

Characters to copy : ©   Select   Copy

4 Click the Font drop-down box to select a different font from the list, for example Wingdings

8 Digital Lifestyle

Windows 10 covers a range of entertainment with the Photos, Groove Music and Movies & TV apps. This chapter shows how to work with these apps and also the online OneDrive function for backing up content.

Using OneDrive

Cloud computing is now a mainstream part of our online experience. This involves saving content to an online server connected to the service that you are using, i.e. through your Microsoft Account. You can then access this content from any computer, using your account login details, and also share it with other people by giving them access to your Cloud service. It can also be used to back up your files, in case they get corrupted or damaged on your PC.

The Cloud service with Windows 10 is known as OneDrive, and you can use it providing that you have a Microsoft Account.

Click on these buttons on the right-hand side of the OneDrive toolbar in Step 3 to, from left to right: sort the content; display it with its details; as thumbnails; or with the details pane.

1 Click on the **OneDrive** app on the Start Menu and follow the wizard to sign-in to OneDrive

2 Open File Explorer and click on the **OneDrive** folder to view its contents

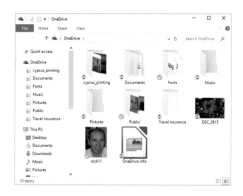

3 To view the contents of OneDrive online, go to the website at **onedrive.live.com** and sign in with your Microsoft Account details. Your OneDrive content is the same as in your OneDrive folder on your computer. Click on items to open, view and edit them

Click on these buttons on the left-hand side of the OneDrive toolbar in Step 3 to, from left to right: create new folders in the file structure, and upload files from other locations.

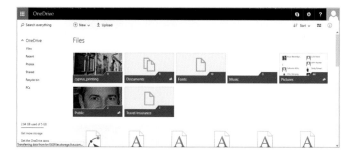

OneDrive Settings

A range of settings can be applied to OneDrive, including adding and syncing folders. To do this:

1 Right-click on the OneDrive icon on the Notification area of the Taskbar and click on **Settings**

2 Click on the **Settings** tab for options for starting OneDrive when you sign in, and for unlinking your OneDrive so that it does not sync with the online function

3 Click on the **Account** tab and click on the **Choose folders** button to select the folder from your computer that you want to sync with your OneDrive account

4 Click on the **OK** button to apply any changes to the OneDrive settings

Hot tip

If the OneDrive icon is not visible on the Notification area of the Taskbar open the **Settings** app and select **Personalization**. Click on **Taskbar** and click on the **Select which icons appear on the taskbar** link. For the **Microsoft OneDrive** option, drag the button to **On**.

Adding Files to OneDrive

OneDrive is built into the file structure of Windows 10 and as well as adding files from OneDrive itself, it is also possible to add them to the OneDrive folder from your computer. Once this has been done, the files can be accessed from OneDrive from your computer, online or any compatible device, using your Microsoft Account login details.

Adding from File Explorer

To add files from File Explorer:

1

In File Explorer, the OneDrive folder is located underneath Quick access

Your OneDrive folder can be pinned to the Quick access section in File Explorer. To do this, right-click on the OneDrive icon in File Explorer and click on **Pin to Quick access**.

2

Click on the OneDrive folder to view its contents

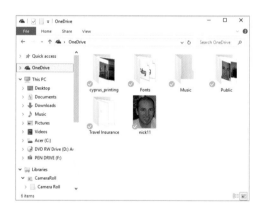

By default, you get 5GB of free OneDrive storage space with Windows 10 (the free allowance was reduced from 15GB in July 2016). This is an excellent way to back up your important documents, since they are stored away from your computer. For up-to-date information on plan allowances and pricing, visit https://onedrive.live.com/about/plans/

3

Add files to the OneDrive folder by dragging and dropping them from another folder or by using Copy and Paste

4 The new content is
available from the
OneDrive app and
also online from your
OneDrive account

Saving files to OneDrive
Files can also be saved directly to OneDrive when they are
created. To do this:

 1 Open a new file in
any app and create the
required content

2 Select **File** > **Save**
from the menu bar and select a
OneDrive folder into which you
want to save the file

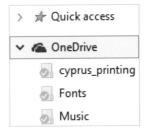

 3 Click on the
Save button

4 The file is saved into the
OneDrive folder and
will be available from
the OneDrive app, and
also online from your
OneDrive account

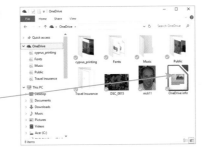

Hot tip

You can share your
Public folder from your
online OneDrive account
by opening it and
clicking or tapping on
the **Share** button. You
can then email the link
to the Public folder to
selected recipients.

163

Viewing Photos

The Photos app can be used to manage and edit your photos, including those stored in your **Pictures** Library. To do this:

1 Click on the **Photos** app on the **Start Menu**

2 Click here to expand and contract the Photos app's menu

To import photos into the Photos app, click on this button on the top toolbar and select the location from where you want to import the photos. This can be a folder on your own computer; a camera or pen drive attached with a USB cable; or a memory card from a camera inserted into a card reader.

3 Click on the **Collection** button to view all of the photos in the Photos app, arranged by date. Scroll up and down to view the photos

4 Click on the **Albums** button to view photos from specific albums. This includes the Camera Roll

Beware

The albums displayed are taken from those stored in the specific folders in File Explorer (by default, the Pictures library). However, the Photos app displays what it thinks are the best photos in the folder, thus creating its own albums.

165

5 Click on the **Camera roll** album to view photos that have been taken with your computer's camera (or copied into this folder from another location)

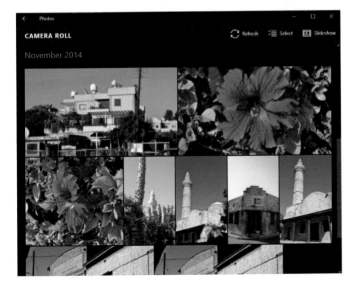

Hot tip

To include an existing folder in the Camera roll, right-click on it in File Explorer and click on **Include in library** > **Camera Roll** from the menu.

...cont'd

6 Within the Albums section, double-click on an album to view its contents. The first photo is also displayed as a banner at the top of the album

7 Double-click on a photo within an album, or collection, to view it at full size. Move the cursor over the photo and click on the left and right arrows (if available) to move through an album or collection

Hot tip

Click on this button to view photos at actual size.

8 Move the cursor over the bottom right-hand corner and click on the + or - symbols to zoom in or out on a photo

...cont'd

Selecting photos

Photos within either a collection or an album in the Photos app can be selected and then shared with other people in various ways, or deleted. To do this:

 In Collections, or an open Album, click on the Select button at the top of the Photos toolbar

 Click here to select a photo or photos

Click on the **Share** button to share the selected photo(s)

Click on one of the options for sharing the selected photo(s)

Alternatively, click on the **Copy** button in Step 3 so that they can be pasted into another app

Don't forget

Click on the **Delete** button from the top toolbar when a photo is selected to delete it.

Editing Photos

In Windows 10 the Photos app now has a range of editing functions so that you can improve and enhance your photos. To use these:

 Open a photo at full size and click on this button to apply auto-enhance editing effects

 Click on the **Edit** button on the top toolbar to access additional editing options. Click on one of the buttons on the left-hand side to view the options on the right-hand side

3 For the **Basic fixes** option, click on one of the buttons at the right-hand side of the screen to apply that effect to the photo, including Enhance, Rotate, Crop, Straighten, Red eye and Retouch

4 For the **Crop** option in Step 3, drag the resizing handles at the corner of the photo to select the area that you want to keep. The area outside the crop guidelines will be removed

Hot tip

Most photos benefit from some degree of cropping, so that the main subject is given greater prominence by removing unwanted items in the background.

...cont'd

5 For the **Filters** option, click on one of the filter effects to apply that to the current photo

Don't forget

It is always worth editing the brightness and contrast of a photo, if only to see if you like the effect. If not, you can undo the action (see Step 11 on the next page).

6 For the **Light** option, click on one of the options at the right-hand side to edit the Brightness, Contrast, Highlights and Shadows of the photo

7 For the **Color** option, click on one of the options at the right-hand side to edit the Temperature, Tint, Saturation and Color boost in the photo

8 For the **Effects** option, click on one of the options at the right-hand side to create a Vignette or a Selective focus effect

9 For the **Vignette** effect, a circular drop-shadow border is created around the photo, to give it an artistic effect

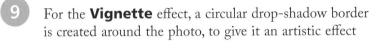

Selective focus enables areas of a photo to be blurred, to create an artistic effect and highlight the main subject. In traditional photography this is known as "depth of field".

10 For the **Light**, **Color** and **Effects** options, drag around this circle to apply the effect to a varying degree

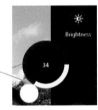

11 Click on the **Undo** button to go back one step in the editing process

12 Click on these buttons to, from left to right, save a copy of the edited photo, apply the changes to the original or cancel the editing changes

171

Groove Music App

The Groove Music app is used to access music that you have added to your computer and also the Music section of the Windows Store, where you can preview, buy and download more music.

1 Click on the **Groove Music** app on the Start menu

2 Click on the Menu button to expand the menu so that the titles are visible, not just the icons

3 Click on a category to view those items

Scroll up and down to view the rest of the available content in the Music section of the Windows Store.

4 Click on the **Get music in Store** button to access the Music section of the Windows Store

5 Browse through the store using the categories in the main window. Click on an item to preview it

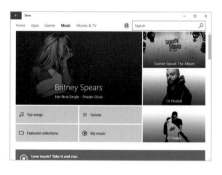

Music that has been bought in the Music section of the Windows Store is then available to be played within the Groove Music app.

6 Once you have selected an item, you can preview individual tracks, view information about the artist and buy albums or specific tracks

Playing Music

Playing your own music

Music that has been added to your computer can be played through the Groove Music app, and you can automatically specify new music to be included when it is added. To do this:

1 Open the Groove Music app and click on either the **Albums**, **Artists**, or **Songs** buttons

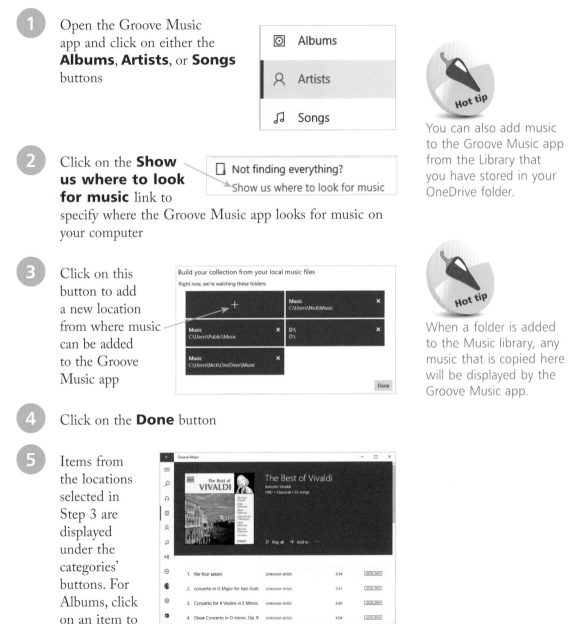

2 Click on the **Show us where to look for music** link to specify where the Groove Music app looks for music on your computer

3 Click on this button to add a new location from where music can be added to the Groove Music app

4 Click on the **Done** button

5 Items from the locations selected in Step 3 are displayed under the categories' buttons. For Albums, click on an item to view all of its tracks

...cont'd

6 Double-click on an individual track to play it, or click on the **Play all** button to play a whole album

7 This button is displayed next to the currently playing track, and its details are displayed at the bottom of the Groove Music app's window

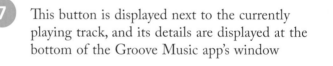

8 Click the speaker button and then drag this button to adjust the volume of a track

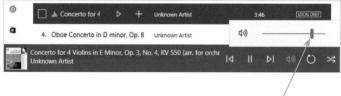

9 Use these buttons above to, from left to right: go to the start of a track; pause/play a track; go to the end of a track; change or mute the volume; shuffle the available tracks; or repeat a track

Viewing Movies and TV

For movie and TV lovers, the Movies & TV app performs a similar function to the Groove Music app. It connects to the Windows Store from where you can preview and buy your favorite movies and TV shows.

1 Click on the **Movies & TV** app on the Start menu

2 Click on the Menu button to view the different sections; Movies, TV & Video (in the same way as for the Groove Music app)

3 Click on the **Shop for more** button to access the **Movies & TV** section of the Windows Store

4 Click on an item to see more information, view a preview clip, buy, or rent, and download the movie

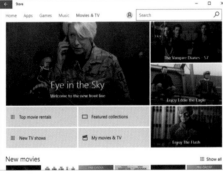

175

By default, DVDs cannot be played on Windows 10 computers. To do this you have to download and buy an enhanced version of the Windows Media Player from the Microsoft website.

You can add your own video clips to the Movies & TV app, from the Videos library in File Explorer, in the same way as adding your own music to the Groove Music app.

Playing Games

The Xbox app can be used with the Xbox 360 games console. It can be used to play games, join friends for multi-player games, watch TV shows and movies, and listen to music. It links to a number of services so that you can access content from websites such as YouTube and Netflix. To use the Xbox app:

1. Click on the **Xbox** app on the Start menu

2. You have to sign in with your Microsoft Account details in order to play Xbox games and interact with other users. Click on the **Sign in** button

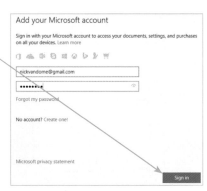

3. Enter your Microsoft Account details and click on the **Sign in** button

Add your Microsoft account

Sign in with your Microsoft account to access your documents, settings, and purchases on all your devices. Learn more

nickvandome@gmail.com

••••••••

Forgot my password

No account? Create one!

Microsoft privacy statement

Sign in

Hot tip

You can also sign in to the Xbox site at **www.xbox.com** to download games and find other people with whom to play games.

4. Click on the **Let's play** button to play games that you have on your PC (and post your scores online), download more games from the Windows Store or play games against other people

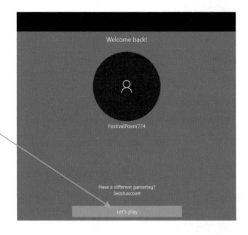

Welcome back!

FestivalPoem774

Have a different gamertag?
Switch account

Let's play

9 Microsoft Edge Browser

Microsoft Edge, designed specifically for Windows 10, is fast and responsive and has a range of innovative features. This chapter looks at how to use the Edge browser to open web pages, use tabs and bookmarks, add notes and graphics to pages and add extensions to increase the overall functionality of the browser.

Internet Connection

Before you can use the internet and browse the web, your computer needs to be set up for connection to the internet. To do this you will require:

Most ISPs also provide additional services such as email accounts, web servers, and storage space on their internet servers for you to create your own website.

- An Internet Service Provider (ISP), to provide an account that gives you access to the internet.

- A transmission network – cable, telephone or wireless.

- Some hardware to link into that transmission network.

- For a broadband connection, such as Digital Subscriber Line (DSL) or cable, you need a DSL or Cable modem or router, usually provided by the ISP.

- For a dial-up connection, you need a dial-up modem, which is usually pre-installed on your computer.

Your ISP may provide software to help you set up your hardware, configure your system and register your ISP account details. However, if you are required to install the connection, or if you are configuring a second connection as a backup, you can use the Set Up a Connection or Network wizard.

Don't forget

It is usually better to use the software and procedures offered by your ISP, if possible, since they will be specifically tailored for the particular service.

1 Access the **Control Panel** and open the **Network and Internet** section, then select the **View network status and tasks** link, under the **Network and Sharing Center** heading

2 Click on the **Set up a new connection or network** link to display the connection options supported

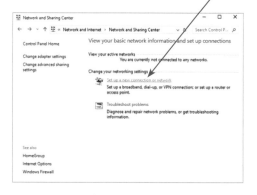

...cont'd

3 Select **Connect to the Internet** and click **Next**

4 The **Connect to the Internet** wizard launches. Select the appropriate connection method from those offered

Windows identifies all of the possible connection methods based on the hardware configuration of your computer. If you have a wireless router or network, you may have an option for wireless connection. If there is no dial-up modem installed, then the Dial-up connection method will not be offered.

Beware

If Windows has already recognized your connection, it detects this. You can select **Browse the Internet now** or **Set up a second connection** (e.g. as a backup).

Don't forget

Continue through the wizard to complete the set-up of your internet connection, ready to start browsing the internet.

Introducing the Edge Browser

The web browser Internet Explorer (IE) has been synonymous with Microsoft for almost as long as the Windows operating system. Introduced in 1995, shortly after Windows 95, it has been the default browser for a generation of web users. However, as with most technologies, the relentless march of time has caught up with IE and, although it is still included with Windows 10, the preferred browser is designed specifically for the digital mobile age. It is called Microsoft Edge and adapts easily to whichever environment it is operating in: desktop, tablet or phone.

The Microsoft Edge browser has a number of performance and speed enhancements compared with IE and it also recognizes that modern web users want a lot more from their browser than simply being able to look at web pages. It includes a function for drawing on and annotating web pages, which can then be sent to other people as screenshots.

There is also a Hub where you can store all of your favorites, downloads and pages that you have selected to read at a later date (which can be when you are offline if required).

Click on this icon from the **Taskbar** or the **Start** menu to open the Microsoft Edge browser at the default Start page.

Internet Explorer can still be used with Windows 10 and it will probably continue to be supported for a considerable period of time.

The Start page also displays news information.

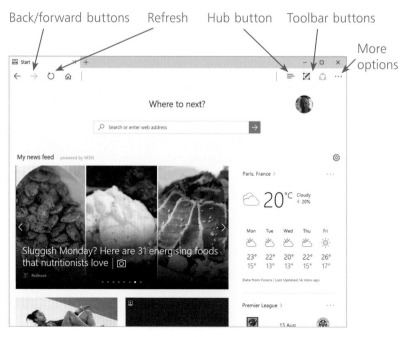

Back/forward buttons   Refresh   Hub button   Toolbar buttons

More options

The Start page can be replaced by your own specific Homepage, see page 182 for details.

180

Smart Address Bar

Smart address bars are now a familiar feature in a lot of modern browsers and Microsoft Edge is no different. This can be used to enter a specific web address, to open that page, or use it to search for a word or phrase. To use the smart address bar:

1 Click anywhere in the Start page address box or in the address box at the top of a web page

2 Start typing a word or website address. As you type, options appear below the address bar. Click on one of the options to go to a specific web page or search for the item

3 Click on one of the options under **Search suggestions** to go to a page with those search results

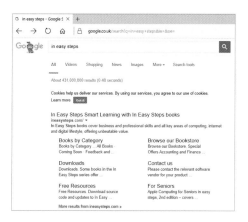

Hot tip

The Personal Digital Assistant, Cortana, can also be used to open web pages, by asking it to open a specific page. The page will be opened in Microsoft Edge.

Hot tip

Search results are found through Microsoft's search engine, Bing. To change the default search engine, first visit the homepage of the search engine you wish to add using Microsoft Edge, then click on **...** **(More Options)** > **Settings**. Then, select the **View advanced settings** button, click on the **Change search engine** button and select a new default search engine.

In the Windows 10 Anniversary Update, the Microsoft Edge browser has a Homepage button on the top toolbar.

Within the settings for Microsoft Edge there is an option for importing favorites from another web browser. To do this, click on the **Import favorites from another browser** button, select the required browser and click on the **Import** button.

If a specific Homepage is assigned, the Start page as shown on page 180 will not be displayed.

Setting a Homepage

By default, Microsoft Edge opens at its own Start page. This may not be ideal for most users, who will want to set their own Homepage that appears when Microsoft Edge is launched.

 Click on this button on the top toolbar to access the menu options

2 Click on the **Settings** button | Settings |

3 By default, the Start page is selected as the opening page

SETTINGS

Choose a theme

| Light ⌄ |

Open Microsoft Edge with

| A specific page or pages ⌄ |

| Enter a URL | 🖫

Open new tabs with

| Top sites and suggested content ⌄ |

Favorites

| View favorites settings |

---

4 Click here and select **A specific page or pages**

Start page

New tab page

Previous pages

A specific page or pages

---

5 Enter the website address you want to use | ineasysteps.com ✕ | 🖫

as your Homepage and click on the **Save** button

Using Tabs

Being able to open several web pages at the same time in different tabs is now a common feature of web browsers. To do this with Microsoft Edge:

 Click on this button at the top of the Microsoft Edge window

 Pages can be opened in new tabs using the smart address bar or the list of **Top sites** that appears below it

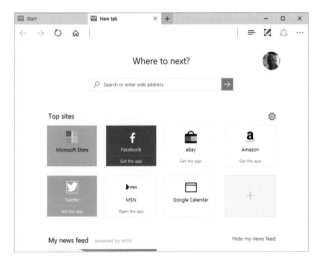

The Start page for new tabs, as displayed in Step 2, can be changed if required. To do this, open the Microsoft Edge Settings as shown on the previous page and change the selection under the **Open new tabs with** heading.

 All open tabs are displayed at the top of the window. Click and hold on a tab to drag it into a new position

Bookmarking Web Pages

Your favorite web pages can be bookmarked so that you can access them with one click from the Hub area, rather than having to enter the web address each time. To do this:

 Open the web page that you want to bookmark

 Click on this button on the toolbar

 Click on the **Favorites** button

 Enter a name for the favorite and where you want it to be saved to (click on the **Create new folder** link if you want to save it to a new location)

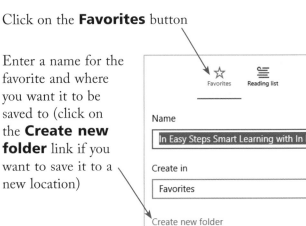

The Favorites bar can be displayed underneath the Address bar by opening the Microsoft Edge Settings and dragging the **Show the favorites bar** button to **On**.

184

 Click on the **Add** button

 The star button turns yellow, indicating that the web page has been added as a Favorite

 Click on this button to access your Favorites (see page 188)

Adding Notes to Web Pages

One of the innovations in the Microsoft Edge browser is the ability to draw on and annotate web pages. This can be useful to highlight parts of a web page or add your own comments and views, which can then be sent to other people. To add notes:

 Open a web page to which you want to add a note or draw on, and click on this button on the toolbar of the Microsoft Edge browser

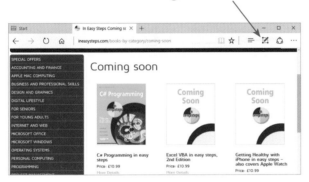

 Click on one of the pen options

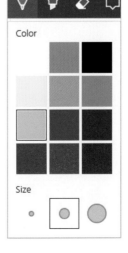 Click on the small triangle in the bottom right-hand corner to select formatting and shape options for the pen

Don't forget

Click on this button on the Notes toolbar to create a web clipping. This an area of a web page that is selected by dragging over it to make the selection. Web clippings can be shared in the same way as notes.

Don't forget

Click on this button on the Notes toolbar to Save a web note or clipping. These can then be accessed from the Favorites section of Microsoft Edge (see page 188).

...cont'd

 Click and drag on the web page to draw over it

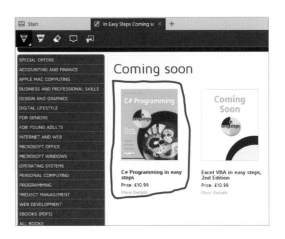

 Click on the eraser icon and drag over any items that you have drawn to remove them, or part of them

 Click on the text icon to add your own text

 Drag over the web page to create a text box

 Type the text that you want displayed on the web page

This is the one I mentioned.

 Click and drag here on a text box to move its position in the window

Sharing Notes and Clippings

Once you have created a web note, this can be saved or shared with other people. There is also an option for selecting part of a web page and sharing this too.

Sharing a web note

To share a web note with other people:

 Once the web note is finished, click on this button on the toolbar for sharing options

 Select an app with which you want to share the web note

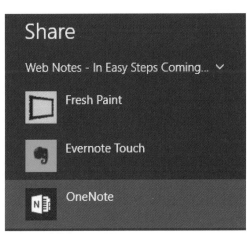

The process for sharing a web clipping is the same as for a web note.

3 The web note is displayed in the selected app

4 Click on the **Send** button to send the web note to the app

Organizing with the Hub

The Hub is the area where you can store a variety of items for the Microsoft Edge browser; from your favorite web pages to pages that you want to read offline at a later date. To use the Hub:

1 Click on this button to open the Hub

2 Click on this button to view your Favorites. Click on one to go to that page

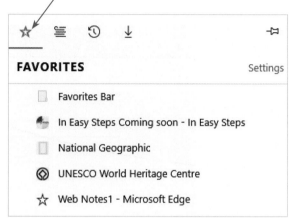

188

3 Click on this button to view your Reading List of pages that you have saved to read offline, or at a later date

4 Click on this button to view your web browsing history

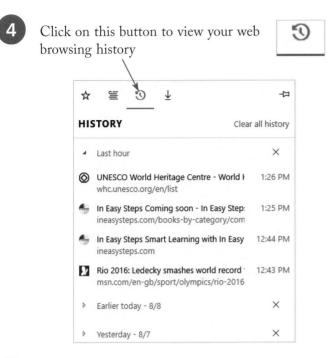

Browsing data can also be cleared from within Microsoft Edge settings. Under **Clear browsing data**, click on the **Choose what to clear** button, check **On** all of the items you want to clear and click on the **Clear** button.

5 Click on **Clear all history** to remove the items in the history

Clear all history

6 Click on this button to view items that you have downloaded from the web, such as PDF documents or apps (although not those from the Windows Store)

Reading List

With some web pages you may want to save the content so that you can read it at a later date. If you make the page a favorite, the content could change the next time you look at it. Instead, you can add the page to your Reading List to ensure that you can read the same content. Also, you have the advantage of being able to access the items in your Reading List when you are offline and not connected to the internet. To do this:

1 Open the web page that you want to add to the Reading List

2 Click on this button on the Microsoft Edge toolbar

3 Click on the **Reading list** button

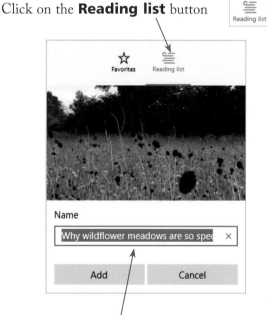

Hot tip

The Reading List is an excellent option if you are traveling and do not have internet access. You can save numerous articles in the Reading List and access them even when you are offline.

190

4 Enter a name for the item and click on the **Add** button

5 Click on this button within the Hub to access and view your Reading List items

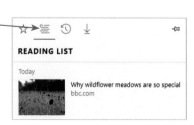

Reading View

Modern web pages contain a lot more items than just text and pictures: video clips, pop-up ads, banners and more contribute to the multimedia effect on many web pages. At times this additional content can enhance the page, but a lot of the time it is a distraction. If you want to just concentrate on the main item on a web page you can do this with the Reading View function:

1 Open the web page that you want to view in Reading View

2 Click on this button on the Microsoft Edge toolbar

3 The text and pictures are presented on a new page, with any additional content removed

Discoveries InsectHow the humble fruit fly is answering life's big questions

How the humble fruit fly is answering life's big questions

By Tom Bonnett 27 July 2016
bbc.com

"Time flies like an arrow; fruit flies like a banana."

It's a phrase loved by linguists to show how a sentence can be read in multiple ways. It also holds truth about the common fruit fly, *Drosophila melanogaster*, which has been studied by scientists for more than 100 years.

4 Click on this button again to return to the standard page view

Beware

Not all web pages support the Reading View functionality. If it is not supported, the button in Step 2 will be grayed-out.

More extensions are added to the Windows Store on a regular basis, so check for them periodically.

Adding Extensions

The Windows 10 Anniversary Update extends the functionality of the Microsoft Edge browser through the inclusion of extensions. These are apps that can be added to the browser to provide a range of functions, such as blocking ads from websites, to including quick links to apps such as Pinterest and Amazon. To add extensions to the Microsoft Edge browser:

 Click on the **More Options** button

 Click on the **Extensions** button

Extensions

 Click on the **Get extensions from the Store** button, to go the Windows Store

EXTENSIONS

Once you add an extension, it'll appear here.

Get extensions from the Store

 The extensions for the Microsoft Edge browser are automatically displayed on the Windows Store page. Click on an extension to view its details

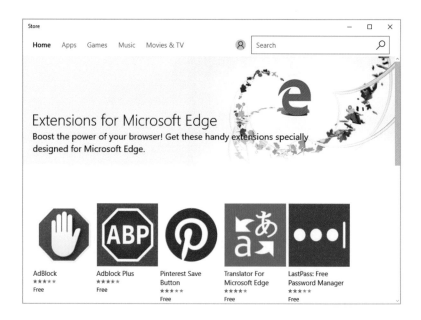

5 Review the details about the extension and click on the **Free** (or price) button to download it

Pinterest Save Button

Pinterest

★★★☆☆

Free

| Free |

+ This product is an extension for: Microsoft Edge

6 Once the extension has been downloaded, you will be prompted to turn it on to start using it. Click on the **Turn it on** button

> You have a new extension
>
> To start using Pin It Button, turn it on. This extension is allowed to:
>
> • Read and change content on websites you visit
> • Read and change your cookies
> • See the websites you visit
> • Store personal browsing data on your device
>
> | Turn it on | Keep it off |

7 Click on the **More Options** button   · · ·

8 The newly downloaded extension is displayed. Right-click on it and click on the **Show next to address bar** button

> Pin It
>
> _____ Show next to address bar
>
> New window   Manage

Hot tip

To remove an extension, right-click on it on the toolbar and click on the **Manage** button. In the next window, click on the **Uninstall** button.

9 The extension is displayed on the top toolbar, next to the More Options button

More Options

There is no traditional menu bar in Microsoft Edge, but more options can be accessed from the right-hand toolbar:

 Click on this button to access the options

 Click here to open a new browsing window, or a **New InPrivate window** which does not record any of your browsing history

The full range of Microsoft Edge **Settings** can be accessed from the **... (More Options)** button.

Hot tip

Some web page functionality does not yet work in Microsoft Edge, so **Open with Internet Explorer** is a useful option.

New window

New InPrivate window

Zoom   —   100%   +

Cast media to device

Find on page

Print

Pin this page to Start

F12 Developer Tools

Open with Internet Explorer

Send feedback

Extensions

What's new and tips

Settings

3 Click on the **Zoom** button to increase or decrease the magnification of the page being viewed

4 Click on the **Find on page** button to search for a specific word or phrase on the web page

5 Click on the **Print** button to print the current web page

6 Click on the **Open with Internet Explorer** button to open the current web page in Microsoft Edge's predecessor

10 Keeping in Touch

This chapter looks at communicating via the Mail, People, Skype and Calendar apps.

Setting Up Mail

Email has become an essential part of everyday life, both socially and in the business world. Windows 10 accommodates this with the Mail app. This can be used to link to online services such as Gmail and Outlook (the renamed version of Hotmail) and also other email accounts. To set up an email account with Mail:

1 Click on the **Mail** app on the Start menu

2 Click on the **Accounts** button

3 Click on the **Add account** button

4 Select the type of account to which you want to link via the Mail app. This can be an online email account that you have already set up

Hot tip

The **Other account** option in Step 4 can be used to add a non-webmail account. This is usually a POP3 account and you will need your email address, username, password, and usually the incoming and outgoing email servers. If you do not know these they should be supplied by your email provider. They should also be available in the Account settings of the email account you want to add to the Mail app.

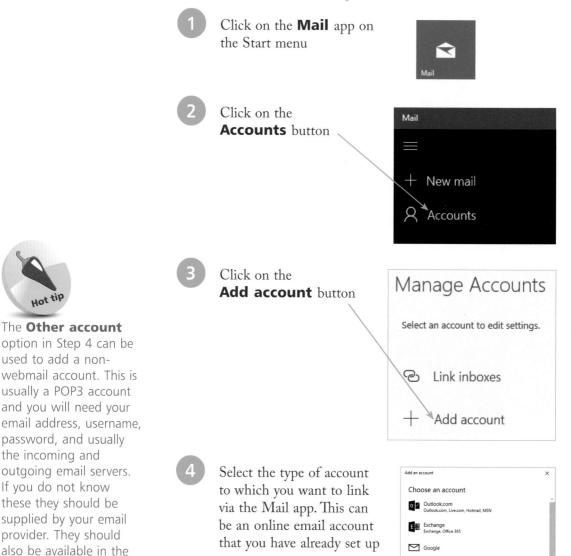

5 Enter your current sign in details for the selected email account and click on the **Sign in** button

6 Once it has been connected, the details of the account are shown under the Mail heading, including the mailboxes within the account. Click on the **Inbox** to view the emails within it

7 The list of emails appears in the main window. Double-click on an email to view it at full size

You can add more than one account to the Mail app. If you do this you will be able to select the different accounts to view within Mail.

Working with Mail

Once you have set up an account in the Mail app you can then start creating and managing your emails with it.

 On the Inbox page, open an email and click on the **Reply**, **Reply all** or **Forward** buttons to respond

 Open an email and click on the **Delete** button to remove it

Composing email

To compose and send an email message:

1 Click on this button to create a new message

2 Click in the **To** field and enter an email address

3 Click on the **Cc & Bcc** link to access options for blind copying

4 The email address can either be in the format of myname@email.com or enter the name of one of your contacts from the People app and the email address will be entered automatically

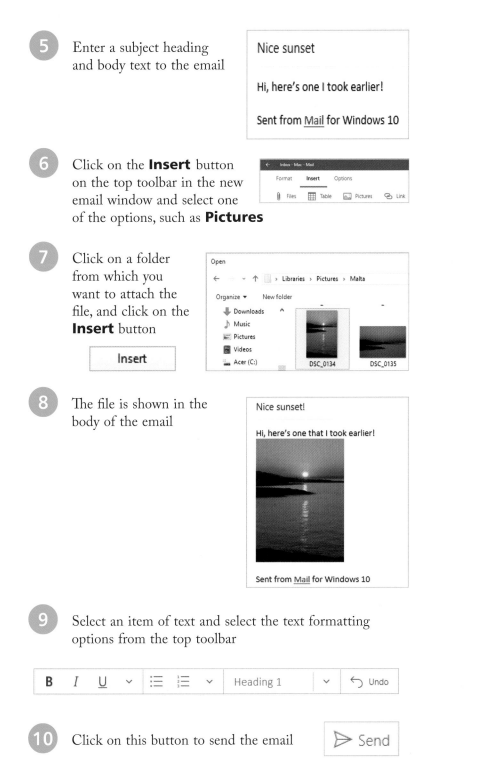

5 Enter a subject heading and body text to the email

Nice sunset

Hi, here's one I took earlier!

Sent from Mail for Windows 10

6 Click on the **Insert** button on the top toolbar in the new email window and select one of the options, such as **Pictures**

Inbox - Mac - Mail

Format   Insert   Options

Files   Table   Pictures   Link

7 Click on a folder from which you want to attach the file, and click on the **Insert** button

Insert

Open

> Libraries > Pictures > Malta

Organize ▼   New folder

Downloads
Music
Pictures
Videos
Acer (C:)

DSC_0134   DSC_0135

8 The file is shown in the body of the email

Nice sunset!

Hi, here's one that I took earlier!

Sent from Mail for Windows 10

9 Select an item of text and select the text formatting options from the top toolbar

B   *I*   U̲   ⌄   ☰   ☰   ⌄   Heading 1   ⌄   ↶ Undo

10 Click on this button to send the email

▷ Send

Finding People

An electronic address book is always a good feature to have on a computer, and with Windows 10 this function is provided by the People app. This not only allows you to add your own contacts manually, you can also link to any of your online accounts, such as Facebook, Twitter and LinkedIn, and import the contacts that you have there. To do this:

1 Click on the **People** app on the Start menu

2 The current contacts are displayed. By default, these will be linked to your Microsoft Account, if you have created one

Hot tip

You can also select accounts to add to the People app from the Homepage when you first open it.

3 Click on the **Settings** button to add new accounts from which you want to import contacts

4 Click on the **Add an account** button

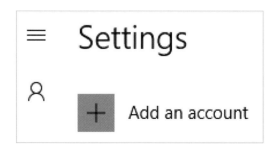

5 Select the account or service from which you would like to import your contacts

Choose an account

O Outlook.com
Outlook.com, Live.com, Hotmail, MSN

E Exchange
Exchange, Office 365

✉ Google

✉ iCloud

⚙ Advanced setup

Close

6 Enter your sign in details for the selected account and click on the **Sign in** button

Add an account ✕

iCloud

Email address

nickvandome@mac.com ✕

Send your messages using this name

Nick

Password

●●●●●●●

We'll save this information, so you don't have to sign in every time.

Cancel   Sign in

7 A confirmation window informs you that the account has been set up and linked to the People app. Click on the **Done** button

All done!

Your account was set up successfully.

✉ nickvandome@mac.com

Done

8 The contacts from the linked account are imported and added under the **Contacts** heading

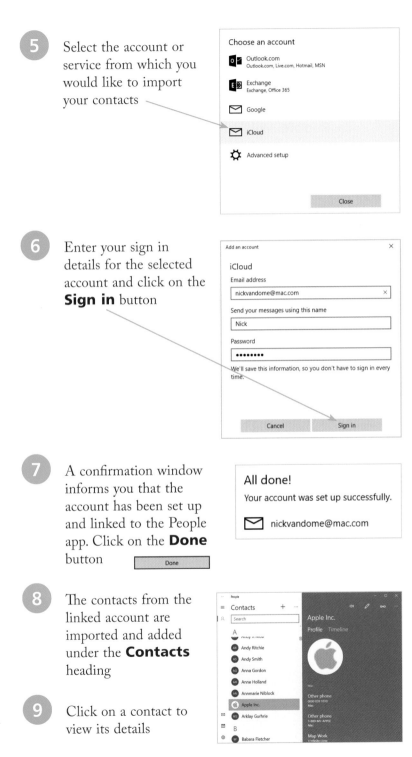

9 Click on a contact to view its details

Don't forget

See page 203 for details about editing an entry.

...cont'd

Adding contacts manually

As well as importing contacts, it is also possible to enter them manually into the People app:

 Click on this button at the top of the **People** app

 Enter details for the new contact, including name, email address and phone number

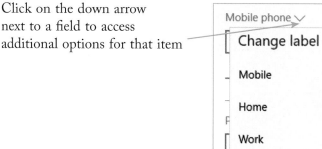

Hot tip

To delete a contact, right-click on their name in the Contacts list and click on the **Delete** button to remove it.

Click on the down arrow next to a field to access additional options for that item

Click on the **Save** button at the top of the window to create the new contact

5 Click on a contact in the Contacts window to view their details

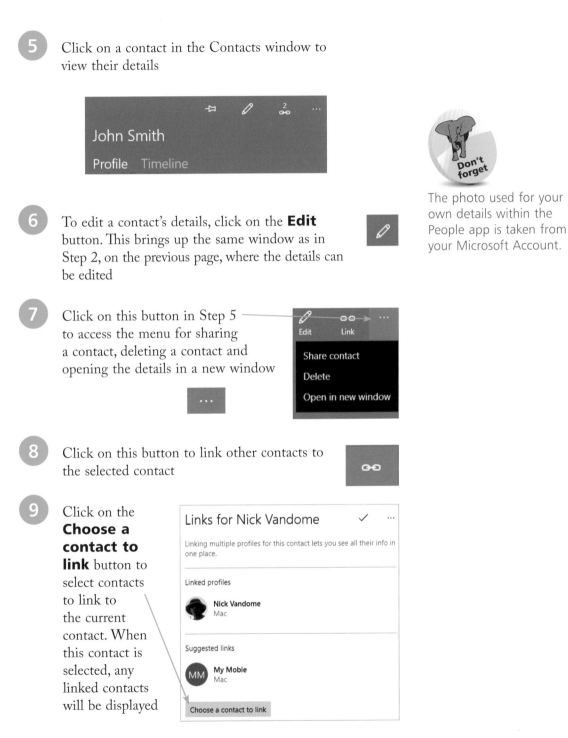

The photo used for your own details within the People app is taken from your Microsoft Account.

6 To edit a contact's details, click on the **Edit** button. This brings up the same window as in Step 2, on the previous page, where the details can be edited

7 Click on this button in Step 5 to access the menu for sharing a contact, deleting a contact and opening the details in a new window

8 Click on this button to link other contacts to the selected contact

9 Click on the **Choose a contact to link** button to select contacts to link to the current contact. When this contact is selected, any linked contacts will be displayed

Chatting with Skype

Skype is one of the premier services for free voice calls (to other Skype users) and instant messaging for text messages. It can now be incorporated into your Windows 10 experience and used to keep in touch with family, friends and work colleagues at home and around the world.

Don't forget

If the Skype button is not available on the Start menu, the app can be downloaded from the Windows Store.

 Click on the **Skype Preview** button on the Start menu

S Skype Preview

 If you already have a Skype account you can sign in with these details, or

Welcome to the Skype Preview

Sign in using your Skype or Microsoft account to experience the next generation of Skype for Windows 10. It's simpler, faster and packed with great new features.

Skype or Microsoft account

Create a new account

with your Microsoft Account details. Click on **Create a new account** to create a new Skype account

 Once you have entered your Skype sign in details you can check your speakers, microphone and webcam, for voice and video calls. Click on the **Sign In** button

Sign In

 Recent conversations are listed in the left-hand panel, or contacts can be selected to start a new conversation (see the next page)

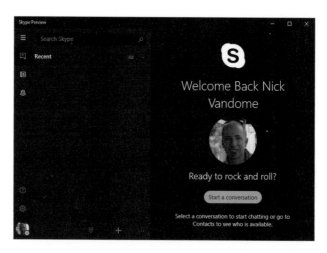

5 Click on this button to view your Skype contacts. Tap on one to start a voice or video call, or a text message

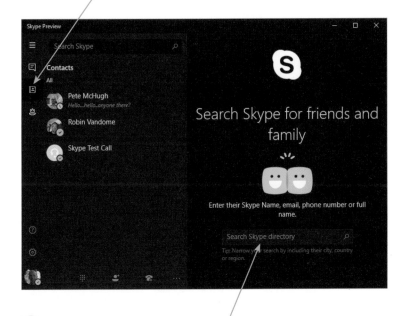

6 Click in the **Search Skype directory** box to look for other Skype contacts

7 Select a contact and click in this box to start a text conversation

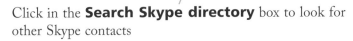

8 Select a contact and click on the phone button to make a voice call, or the video button to make a video call

Don't forget

When you create a text conversation with one of your contacts in Skype, it will continue down the page as you respond to each other.

Don't forget

When you add someone as a contact you have to send them a contact request, which they must accept to become one of your contacts.

Beware

Do not accept requests from people you don't know. If you receive one of these, click on **Decline** to remove the request.

Using the Calendar

The Calendar app can be used to record important events and reminders. To view the calendar:

Accounts can be added to the Calendar app in the same way as for the Mail and People apps.

1 Click on the **Calendar** app on the Start menu, or access it from **All apps**

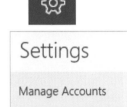

2 Click on the **Settings** button

3 Click on the **Manage Accounts** button to add or delete a calendar account

4 Click here to view specific months and click on the top toolbar to view by **Day**, **Work week**, **Week**, **Month**, **Year** or **Today**

5 Click on these buttons to move between months (or swipe left or right on a touchpad)

...cont'd

Adding events

Events can be added to the calendar and various settings can be applied to them, such as recurrence and reminders.

 Click on a date to create a new event or click on the **New event** button

Reminders can be set for calendar events and these appear in the **Notifications** section. Click on this box on the top toolbar to set a time period for a reminder.

12 hours	∨

2 Enter an **Event name** and a **Location** at the top of the window

Calendar   – □ ✕

Home

Save & Close   Delete   Show As: Free   Reminder: 12 hours   Repeat

← Details   People

Event name   Invite someone

Location   Response   Name

Start: September 10, 2015   12:00 AM ✓ All day   Me

End: September 10, 2015   12:00 AM

Calendar   ∨

Event Description

207

3 Click on the **Start** field and enter a date and time for the event

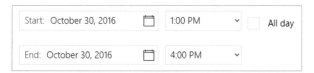

Start: October 30, 2016	📅	1:00 PM	∨	☐ All day
End: October 30, 2016	📅	4:00 PM	∨	

4 If **All day** is selected, the time in the **Start** and **End** fields will be grayed-out

Start: October 30, 2016	📅	12:00 AM	∨	☑ All day
End: October 30, 2016	📅	12:00 AM	∨	

...cont'd

5 For a recurring event, click on this button on the top toolbar

6 Select an option for the recurrence, such as **Weekly** and select a day for the recurrence

Repeat

Start: October 30, 2016   ✕   📅

Weekly   ⌄

Every 1 ⌄ week(s) on

✓ Sun   Mon   Tue   Wed

Thu   Fri   Sat

End: Never   📅

Hot tip

If you have connected the People app to your other accounts, such as Facebook or Twitter, the birthdays of your contacts from these sites will automatically be added to your calendar.

7 Click on the **Save and close** button in the main window to save the event

 Save and close

8 To delete an existing event, move the cursor over it and click on the **Edit occurrence** button

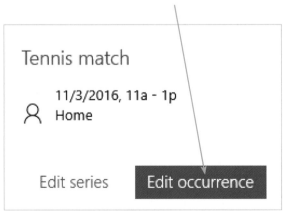

Tennis match

11/3/2016, 11a - 1p
👤 Home

Edit series   Edit occurrence

9 Click on the **Delete** button   🗑 Delete

11 Networking

Windows 10 has a built-in networking capability, so that a variety of items can be shared between two or more computers. This chapter shows how to do this, and how to use the HomeGroup feature for file sharing.

The network adapter can be connected to the USB port, inserted in the PC Card slot or installed inside your computer.

Ethernet adapters connect to a network hub, switch or wired router. Wireless adapters connect through a wireless router or a combination of router/switch.

You may already have some of these elements in operation, if you have an existing network running a previous version of Windows.

Network Components

There are numerous possibilities for setting up a home network. To start with, there are two major network technologies:

- **Wired** – e.g. Ethernet, using twisted pair cables to send data at rates of 10, 100 or 1000 Mbps (megabits per second).

- **Wireless** – using radio waves to send data at rates of 11 or 54 Mbps (or up to, in theory, 300 Mbps with the latest devices).

There is also a variety of hardware items required:

- **Network adapter** – appropriate to the network type, with one for each computer in the network.

- **Network controller** – one or more hub, switch or router, providing the actual connection to each network adapter.

There is also the internet connection (dial-up, DSL or cable), using:

- A modem connected to one of the computers.

- A modem connected to the network.

- Internet access incorporated into the router or switch.

Set Up Your Network

The steps you will need, and the most appropriate sequence to follow, will depend on the specific options on your system. However, the main steps will include:

- Install network adapters in the computers, where necessary.

- Set up or verify the internet connection.

- Configure the wireless router or access point.

- Connect other computers and start up Windows on each PC.

Install hardware

If you need to install a wired or wireless network adapter, follow the instructions provided with the adapter. For example, to install the Linksys Wireless-N USB adapter:

 Insert the CD provided, and the setup program will start up automatically. Select the **Click Here to Start** button

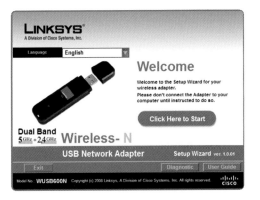

 Follow the instructions (giving permission for access where requested) to complete the software installation

 When prompted, attach the adapter to a USB port, via a cable if needed

 When Windows has detected the wireless networks in range, select your network and click on the **Connect** button

Hot tip

With all the options and combinations that might be available, configuring the network could be complex. However, Windows 10 is designed to automate as much of the task as possible.

Don't forget

Depending on the AutoPlay settings (**Settings** > **Devices** > **AutoPlay**), you may be prompted to run the installation option when you insert the CD.

Beware

Enter the security key for your wireless network when prompted.

Internet Connection

You do not actually require an internet connection to set up a network, if all you want to do is share files and printers. However, in most cases the main purpose of the network is to share your connection to the internet across several computers.

Verify your connection

If you already have an internet connection, open your web browser and go to a website that gets regularly updated (e.g. a news site). If the website opens with up-to-date entries and you don't get an error message, your connection is working.

Install a router

You can use a router with a DSL modem (an internet gateway) to make an internet connection available for sharing. This is usually set up on one computer, connected via an Ethernet cable or a USB cable. A configuration program may be provided on an installation CD or you can use your web browser:

If your router has been installed, Windows will automatically complete the connection to the internet.

1 Open the browser and enter the IP address provided for the router, e.g. 192.168.1.254 or a similar local IP address

If you go to a website that stays relatively static, some of its web pages might be stored on your computer and will display correctly even if your connection is faulty.

 Select **Settings** and enter the administrator username (if required) and password, as provided by your ISP

You will be using the default ID and password for the particular equipment. While this can only be accessed from a direct local connection, you may feel more secure if you change the password.

3 Select **Admin Password**, then enter the old password and the new password and click **Change password**

Don't forget

The options offered will depend on the particular features of your router or gateway device, but they should, in principle, be similar.

4 Select **Wireless** to change the setup, for example by providing a new SSID (Service Set Identifier, the wireless network name) and choosing the encryption type and key

Beware

Do not use the default values for the parameters, since these could be known to other people.

5 You can also change the channels used for the wireless communications if you have problems with network range or speed, or interference from other devices

Discover Networks

You can connect your computers to form a network using Ethernet cables and adapters, or by setting up your wireless adapters and routers. When you start up each computer, Windows 10 will examine the current configuration and discover any new networks that have been established since the last start up. You can check this, or connect manually to a network, from within the default settings from the Network & Internet section of Settings. To do this:

 Click on the **Settings** app and click on the **Network & Internet** button

Network & Internet
Wi-Fi, airplane mode, VPN

 Drag the Wi-Fi button to **On**. Under the **Wi-Fi** heading, click on one of the available networks

 Click on the network and drag **On** the **Connect automatically when in range** box

⚙ PlusnetWireless792287

Connect automatically when in range

⬤ On

 The selected network is shown as **Connected**. This is also shown in the Notifications area

Wi-Fi

⬤ On

PlusnetWireless792287
Connected, secured

If your network is unavailable for any reason, this will be noted in Step 2.

214

Network and Sharing Center

The Network and Sharing Center within the Control Panel is where you can view settings for your network.

1 To open the Network and Sharing Center, access the Control Panel and click on the **Network and Internet** link

Network and Internet
View network status and tasks
Choose homegroup and sharing options

215

Don't forget

The Network and Sharing Center displays network settings and provides access to networking tasks on the computer.

2 Click on the **Network and Sharing Center** link

Network and Sharing Center
View network status and tasks | Connect to a network
View network computers and devices

HomeGroup
Choose homegroup and sharing options

Internet Options
Change your homepage | Manage browser add-ons
Delete browsing history and cookies

3 Details of the current network are displayed in the Network and Sharing Center

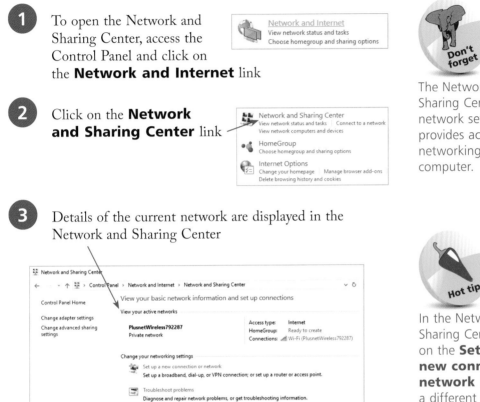

Hot tip

In the Network and Sharing Center, click on the **Set up a new connection or network** link to create a different network from the one currently in use.

4 Click on the link shown next to **Connections:** to see details of your Wi-Fi connection

Access type: Internet
HomeGroup: Ready to create
Connections: Wi-Fi (PlusnetWireless792287)

5 The Wi-Fi information is displayed. Click on the **Properties** button for more information

Join the HomeGroup

The HomeGroup is a network function that enables a Windows 10 computer to connect to another Windows 10 machine (or Windows 7/8) and share content. You can set up and connect to the HomeGroup through the Control Panel:

1 Access **Network and Internet** in the Control Panel and click on the **HomeGroup** link

2 Click on the **Create a homegroup** button to start setting up the HomeGroup

3 Click the **Next** button

4 Select the items that you want to share in the HomeGroup and click on the **Next** button

5 Enter the password that has to be provided from the other computer. Click on the **Finish** button. Once you have joined the HomeGroup you will be able to share your files on the other computer, and vice versa

Don't forget

When you add a computer to your network, Windows 10 on that computer will detect that there is a HomeGroup already created.

Beware

A HomeGroup applies to any user with an account on the computer, so if a different user logs on, the associated files will also be accessible.

Don't forget

Windows generates the password when the HomeGroup is created. If you forget the password, you can find it in the Control Panel on any computer already joined to the HomeGroup.

Sharing Files and Folders

There are different ways in which you can share items once a HomeGroup has been set up:

 Open File Explorer and select the **HomeGroup** in the Navigation pane, then click on the **Share libraries and devices** button in the HomeGroup section of the File Explorer Ribbon tabs

 Select the items that you want to share with the HomeGroup. This will be done automatically, i.e. if you share Pictures then all of the items in the Pictures library will be shared, as will new ones that are added in the future

The Share with section in File Explorer is accessed from the Share tab on the Ribbon.

Don't forget

3️⃣ To share a specific item, select it in File Explorer and click on the **HomeGroup (view)** button in the Share with section

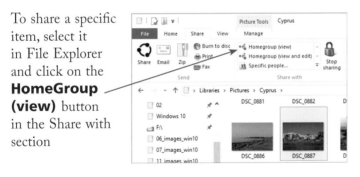

4️⃣ Select HomeGroup in the Navigation pane of the File Explorer pane to view the shared item in Step 3

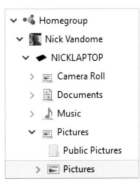

Sharing Settings

Within the Network and Sharing Center there are also options for specifying how items are shared over the network, not just in the HomeGroup. To select these:

 Open the Network and Sharing Center and click on the **Change advanced sharing settings** link

> Change advanced sharing settings

 Select sharing options for different networks, including Private, Guest or Public and All networks. Options can be selected for turning on network discovery so that your computer can see other computers on the network, and file and printer sharing

Don't forget

If you are sharing over a network you should be able to access the Public folder on another computer (providing that network discovery is turned on). If you are the administrator of the other computer you will also be able to access your own Home folder, although you will need to enter the required password for this (see page 216).

Click on these arrows to expand the options for each network category

View Network Components

You can also view the components of the network in File Explorer. To do this:

1 Open File Explorer and click on the **Network** library

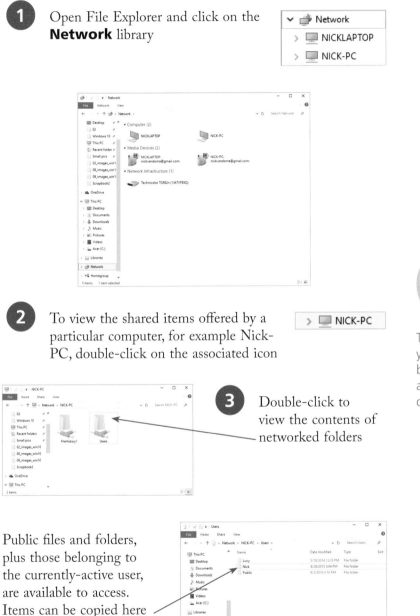

2 To view the shared items offered by a particular computer, for example Nick-PC, double-click on the associated icon

3 Double-click to view the contents of networked folders

Public files and folders, plus those belonging to the currently-active user, are available to access. Items can be copied here for sharing purposes.

Don't forget

The Public folder on your own computer can be used to make items available to other users on the network.

Network Troubleshooting

 1 Open the Network and
Sharing Center and
select **Troubleshoot
problems**

> Troubleshoot problems
> Diagnose and repair network problems, or get
> troubleshooting information.

Don't forget

Windows 10 provides
several troubleshooters
to resolve common
problems with networks.
They are downloaded, so
you can always get the
most up-to-date help.

2 Windows searches online for troubleshooting packs

Network and Internet — □ ×

← → ∨ ↑ 🖼 « Troublesho... › Network and Internet ∨ ↻ Search Troublesh... 🔎

Troubleshoot problems - Network and Internet

Network

Internet Connections
Find and fix problems with connecting to the Internet or to websites.

Shared Folders
Find and fix problems with accessing files and folders on other computers.

HomeGroup
Find and fix problems with viewing computers or shared files in a homegroup.

Network Adapter
Find and fix problems with wireless and other network adapters.

Incoming Connections
Find and fix problems with incoming computer connections and Windows Firewall.

Printing

Printer
Find and fix problems with printing.

3 Select, for example, Shared Folders and follow the
prompts to find and hopefully resolve the problems

Hot tip

In this case, a problem
accessing a folder on
another computer is
quickly resolved as a
typing error, when
Windows says it cannot
find "windows10" but
detects the similar folder
name "Windows 10"
(with a space before 10).

×

← 🖼 Shared Folders

Troubleshoot and help prevent computer problems

Shared Folders
Find and fix problems with accessing files and folders on other computers.

Advanced

Publisher: Microsoft Corporation
Privacy statement

Next   Cancel

220

12 System and Security

Windows 10 includes tools to help maintain your hard drive, protect your computer from malicious software, back up your files, folders and apps, and keep your system up-to-date.

System Properties

There are several ways to open the System Properties, and view information about your computer:

 1 Access the **Control Panel**, **System and Security** and then click on the **System** > **See the name of this computer**

System and Security
Review your computer's status
Save backup copies of your files with File History

System
View amount of RAM and processor speed
Allow remote access
Launch remote assistance
See the name of this computer

2 Press the **WinKey** + the **Pause/Break** keys

3 Right-click **This PC** in the File Explorer Navigation pane, and select **Properties** from the menu

4 Right-click on the **Start** button and select **System** from the context menu

Don't forget

The main System panel provides the Windows 10 edition, processor details, memory size, computer and network names, and Windows 10 activation status. There are also links to the Device Manager and to more advanced settings.

Device Manager

1 Select **Device Manager** to list all of the hardware components that are installed on your computer

2 Select the ❯ symbol to expand that entry to show details

3 Double-click any device to open its properties

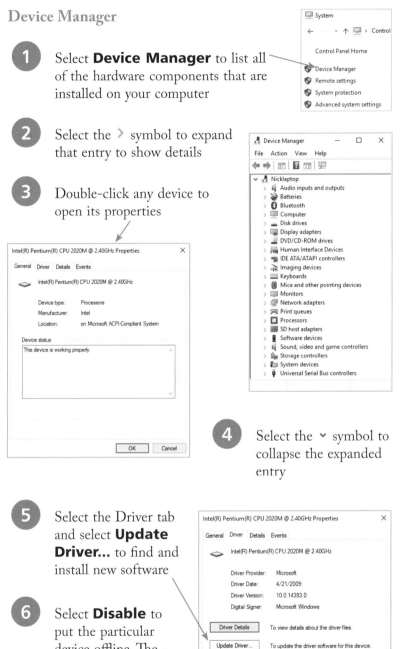

4 Select the ❯ symbol to collapse the expanded entry

5 Select the Driver tab and select **Update Driver...** to find and install new software

6 Select **Disable** to put the particular device offline. The button changes to **Enable**, to reverse the action

You may be prompted for an administrator password or asked for permission to continue, when you select some Device Manager entries.

Click on the **Roll Back Driver...** button to switch back to the previously-installed driver for that device, if the new one fails.

Clean Up Your Disk

1 In File Explorer, right-click the **C:** drive and click on the **Properties** option

2 Click on the **Disk Cleanup** button

3 Disk Cleanup scans the drive to identify files that can be safely removed

You can have more than one hard disk on your computer.

4 All of the possible files are listed by category, and the sets of files recommended to be deleted are marked with a tick symbol

5 Make changes to the selections, clicking **View Files** if necessary to help you choose

6 Select the button **Clean up system files**, to also include these, then select **OK**

7 Deleted files will not be transferred to the Recycle Bin, so confirm that you do want to permanently delete all of these files. The files will be removed and the disk space will become available

...cont'd

When a file is written to the hard disk, it may be stored in several pieces in different places. This fragmentation of disk space can slow down your computer. Disk Defragmenter rearranges the data so the disk will work more efficiently.

1 In the File Explorer, right-click on the **C:** drive and click on the **Properties** option

2 Select the **Tools** tab and click on the **Optimize** button

Don't forget

Spellings are localized.

3 The process runs as a scheduled task, but you can select a drive and select **Analyze** to check out a new drive

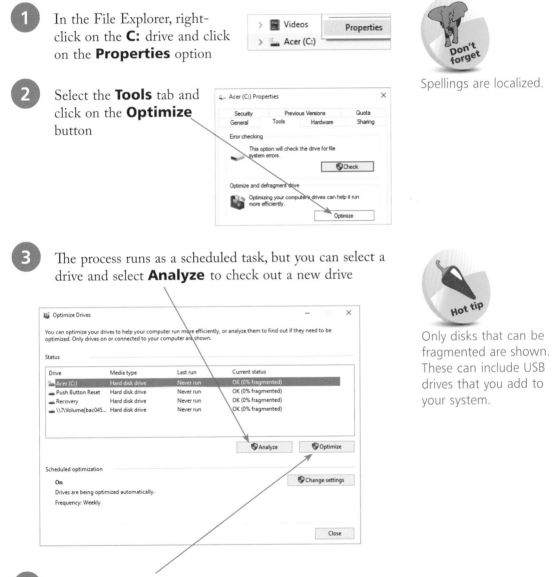

Hot tip

Only disks that can be fragmented are shown. These can include USB drives that you add to your system.

4 Click the **Optimize** button to process the selected disk drive. This may take between several minutes to several hours to complete, depending on the size and state of the disk, but you can still use your computer while the task is running

Windows Update

Updates to Windows 10 and other Microsoft products are supplied regularly, to help prevent or fix problems, improve the security or enhance performance. The way in which they are downloaded and installed can be specified from the Settings app:

1 Access the **Settings** app and click on the **Update & security** button

2 Click on **Windows Update**

Update & security

↻ Windows Update

Hot tip

Click on the **Windows Insider Program** link within the **Update & security** settings to access pre-release versions of the latest Windows 10 updates.

3 Click on the **Check for updates** button to see details of any updates that are waiting to be installed

Update status

Your device is up to date. Last checked: Yesterday, 12:02 PM

Check for updates

Update history

Don't forget

The **Recovery** option in **Update & security** has a **Reset this PC** option that can be used to reinstall Windows and select which files you want to keep.

4 Click on the **Advanced options** button and click on **Choose how updates are delivered** to specify how updates are installed (by default, it is **Automatic**)

Advanced options

← Settings

⚙ Advanced options

Choose how updates are installed

☐ Give me updates for other Microsoft products when I update Windows.

☐ Defer feature updates
Learn more

☐ Use my sign in info to automatically finish setting up my device after an update.
Learn more

Privacy statement

Choose how updates are delivered

Back Up and Recover Data

1 Open the **Control Panel** and select **Save backup copies of your files with File History**, in the **System and Security** category

2 The first time you do this, you can select a drive such as an external hard drive or a network drive. Click on the **Turn on** button to back up copies of your files

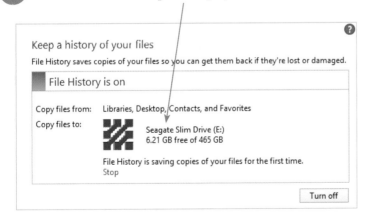

3 Details of the backup are displayed here

4 Click on the **Run now** link to perform another backup

You can also back up files through the Settings app. To do this, select **Settings** > **Update & security** > **Backup** and drag the **Automatically back up my files** button to **On**.

You can create a system image (an exact copy of a drive) and also back up data files in the libraries and other folders on your system.

Items that have been backed up can be recovered through the Control Panel by selecting **System and Security** > **Backup and Restore** > **Restore files from backup**.

System Restore

Windows 10 takes snapshots of the system files before any software updates are applied, or in any event once every seven days. You can also create a snapshot manually. The snapshots are known as Restore Points and are managed by System Restore.

1 From the Control Panel, open **System** under **System and Security** and select **System protection**

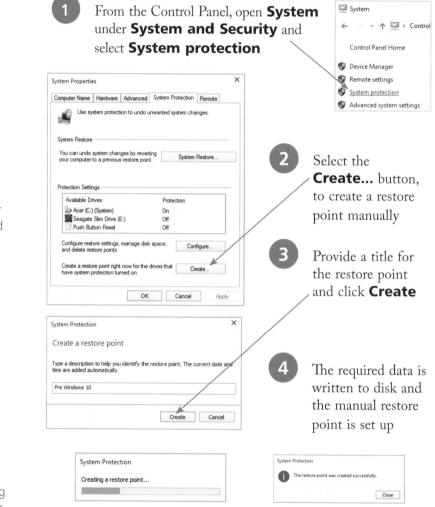

2 Select the **Create...** button, to create a restore point manually

3 Provide a title for the restore point and click **Create**

4 The required data is written to disk and the manual restore point is set up

Hot tip

System Restore returns system files to an earlier point in time, allowing you to undo system changes without affecting your documents, email, and other data files.

228

Beware

System Restore is not intended for protecting personal data files. For these you should use Windows Backup (see page 227).

Using Restore Points

The installation of a new app or driver software may make Windows 10 behave unpredictably or have other unexpected results. Usually, uninstalling the app or rolling back the driver (see page 223) will correct the situation. If this does not fix the problem, use an automatic or manual restore point to reset your system to an earlier date when everything worked correctly.

1 Select **System protection** and click the **System Restore...** button

System Restore...

2 By default this will offer to undo the most recent change. This may fix the problem

System Restore ✕

Restore system files and settings

System Restore can help fix problems that might be making your computer run slowly or stop responding.

System Restore does not affect any of your documents, pictures, or other personal data. Recently installed programs and drivers might be uninstalled.

< Back | Next > | Cancel

Don't forget

You can also run System Restore from Safe Mode, the troubleshooting option. Start up the computer and press **F8** repeatedly as your computer reboots, to display the boot menu, then select **Safe Mode**.

229

3 Otherwise, click **Choose a different restore point**, and pick a suitable time

System Restore ✕

Restore your computer to the state it was in before the selected event

Current time zone: GMT Daylight Time

Date and Time	Description	Type
8/4/2016 12:28:09 PM	Windows Update	Critical Update

Scan for affected programs

< Back | Next > | Cancel

Don't forget

If the selected restore point does not resolve the problem, you can try again, selecting another restore point.

4 Follow the prompts to restart the system using system files from the selected date and time

Security and Maintenance

The Security and Maintenance section in the Control Panel monitors security and delivers alerts for security features.

 In the Control Panel, click on the **Security and Maintenance** link in **System and Security**

> Security and Maintenance
> Review your computer's status and resolve issues
> Change User Account Control settings
> Troubleshoot common computer problems

2 Select the **Change Security and Maintenance settings** link

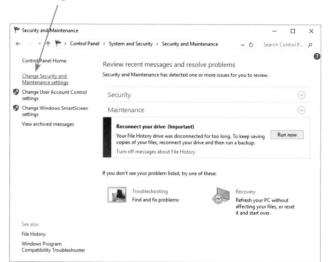

Hot tip

In the Security and Maintenance settings you can also change User Account Control settings, from a link at the side of the window.

3 Check the settings On or Off as required

Windows Firewall

1 Open Control Panel, select the System and Security category and select **Windows Firewall**

2 Select **Turn Windows Firewall on or off** to customize settings for private (home and work) and public networks

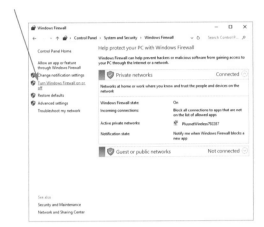

3 Select **Allow an app or feature through Windows Firewall**, to view the allowed apps

Allow an app or feature through Windows Firewall

4 Click on the **Change settings** button to allow or restrict apps

 Change settings

5 Check apps On or Off to allow or remove them from the allowed list. Click on the **OK** button to apply the changes

The Windows Firewall can be used to provide a level of protection against malicious software and viruses.

Firewall is on by default in Windows 10, but you can turn it off if you have another Firewall installed and active.

Only add apps to the allowed list if you are advised to do so by a trusted advisor, or if you trust their origins.

Malware Protection

The Windows Defender app, which is pre-installed with Windows 10, can be used to give a certain amount of protection against viruses and malicious software. To use it:

 Open the Control Panel and type **Windows Defender** into the Search box. Click on the link to open Defender

Windows Defender
Scan for malware and other potentially unwanted software

Malware (malicious software) is designed to deliberately harm your computer. To protect your system, you need up-to-date antivirus and anti-spyware software. Windows Defender provides the latter, but you should install a separate antivirus app.

 For an immediate check, select the **Home** tab and click on the **Scan now** button

 From the **Settings** app, select **Update & security > Windows Defender** and adjust settings such as real-time protection and Cloud-based protection

The Windows Defender version in the Windows 10 Anniversary Update has been enhanced to provide more robust virus protection than earlier versions.